ESSENTIAL
COMPANY LAW

SECOND EDITION

Cavendish
Publishing
Limited

London • Sydney

Titles in the series:

ESSENTIAL COMPANY LAW

SECOND EDITION

Professor Nicholas Bourne
LLB, LLM (Wales), LLM (Cantab), Barrister
Assistant Principal, Swansea Institute

Cavendish
Publishing
Limited

London • Sydney

First published in Great Britain 1994 by Cavendish Publishing Limited, The Glass House, Wharton Street, London WC1X 9PX

Telephone: 071-278 8000   Facsimile: 071-278 8080

e-mail: info@cavendishpublishing.com

Visit our Home Page on http://www.cavendishpublishing.com

Bourne, Nicholas

Company law – 2nd ed – (Essential law series)

1. Corporation law – England 2. Corporation law – Wales

I Title

346.4'2'066

ISBN 1 85941 149 5

Printed and bound in Great Britain

Foreword

This book is part of the Cavendish Essential series. The books in the series are designed to provide useful revision aids for the hard-pressed student. They are not, of course, intended to be substitutes for more detailed treatises. Other textbooks in the Cavendish portfolio must supply these gaps.

The Cavendish Essential series is now in its second edition and is a well-established favourite among students.

The team of authors bring a wealth of lecturing and examining experience to the task in hand. Many of us can even recall what it was like to face law examinations!

Professor Nicholas Bourne
General Editor, Essential Series
Swansea
Summer, 1997

Preface

Essential Company Law provides an attack on the typical company law syllabus for the busy law student. Each chapter sets out, in detail, important areas of company law – areas that are likely to arise in the examination. It also covers other areas in less depth.

Nicholas Bourne
Summer, 1997

Contents

1 The nature of a company and lifting the veil

You should be familiar with the following areas:

- the distinctions between the company and the partnership
- the various classifications of companies, especially the difference between a private and a public company
- the separate personality of the company – the *Salomon* principle
- the statutory exceptions to the *Salomon* principle
- the judicial exceptions to the *Salomon* principle
- a company's responsibility for crimes and torts

Introduction

In this first chapter the aim is to set the scene on key areas of company law. Much of this chapter may not be the subject of a specific examination question but the information contained in the essential notes is vital to an understanding of much of company law. Key issues are dealt with in some detail.

The company and the partnership

When businesspeople set up in business, they will need to consider whether to operate as a partnership or as a company. The two types of business could not, in some ways, be more different. The company is a separate person in law (see *Salomon v Salomon & Co Ltd* (1897)). The company can own property, commit crimes and conclude contracts. The partnership, on the other hand, is no more than a convenient term for describing the sum total of the partners who make up the partnership or firm. The partnership is not a separate person in law. The partnership cannot commit crimes or torts. These can only be committed by the partners, its agents.

A further consequence of the distinction between the company and the partnership is that the company pays corporation tax as a separate entity on its profits whilst the partnership does not pay tax as such, although a tax assessment may be raised against it. The tax is in fact paid under the schedular income tax system by the individual partners in the firm.

Advantages of incorporation

The company has access to limited liability. Not all companies are limited. Indeed, there are many unlimited companies where liability of the members is not limited. The advantage of such companies is that they do not need to file annual accounts. By contrast, although there is such a thing as a limited partnership, in practice partnerships are unable to limit the liability of all of the partners.

The company can separate ownership from control. The people who subscribe for the shares do not necessarily have any hand in the running of the business. This will be particularly true of a large quoted company, eg Lloyds Bank Plc. In the case of the partnership, the partners of the firm are agents and are able to act to bind the firm and are bound by the actions of the other partners.

Since the company is a separate entity, in theory it could go on for ever. Many companies have a long pedigree, eg the Tenby & County Club Ltd, set up in 1876. Partnerships have to be reformed and reconstituted upon the death or bankruptcy of individual partners.

Where a person wishes to invest money and needs the investment to be readily realisable, the company is the appropriate vehicle. This is particularly true if the company is quoted since there is then a market mechanism for disposing of the shares of the business. In a partnership, it is likely that a partnership share will be much less easily realisable than shares in a company.

A further advantage for the company is in the context of raising finance. A company, again as it is a separate entity, is able to mortgage all of its assets by way of a floating charge to secure a borrowing from, for example, a bank. This means of securing a loan and raising finance is not available to the partnership.

The costs of incorporation are minimal. On the other hand, there are certain hidden costs involved in incorporation. These costs would include the legal costs of setting the company up and the annual on-going costs of preparing company accounts, there are also many formalities connected with setting up and running a company. In addition to the constitution of the company, there is a plethora of company forms that have to be filed in relation to the management of the company, shares issued by the company, debentures issued by the company, and charges created by the company. The annual return has to be filed every year. Furthermore, the company is obliged to keep a series of company books at the company's registered office or some other appropriate place. These registers would include the register of members, register of directors and register of charges.

An important consideration for the entrepreneurs who are setting up in business is what the tax consequences of setting up as a company or as a partnership will be. It is not possible to say that the balance of advantage always lies with one form of business rather than another but it will certainly be a powerful consideration when the entrepreneurs are weighing the relative advantages and disadvantages of each form of business medium.

The information set out above in relation to different types of business is extremely important background information in tackling company law questions and understanding why people set up as companies rather than operating a business through the medium of a partnership. Before concluding this particular point, it is worth noting that s 716 of the Companies Act 1985 provides that in relation to trading businesses the maximum number of partners that may be involved in the firm is set at 20 so that if it is desired to involve in excess of 20 people in the management of the business, it is appropriate to form a company. The section does not apply to a large number of professional businesses which are exempted from it, eg solicitors.

Public companies and private companies

Another key area which permeates the whole of company law is the distinction between the public company and the private company. The vast majority of companies are private companies. Those that hit the news headlines tend, however, to be public and this may give a distorted view of the numerical significance of public companies.

The surprising feature of British company law is that, with relatively few exceptions, the same rules apply to public companies as to private companies.

The second EC Directive on company law did, however, lead to a re-writing of the distinction in British company law and entail some new distinctions to be drawn in the Companies Act 1980 (now consolidated into the Companies Act 1985).

A public company must have a minimum subscribed share capital of at least £50,000 paid up to at least 25% before it can be incorporated. This was a requirement of the Second EC Directive which set the minimum subscribed share capital for public companies within the European Community at 25,000 ECU. In addition to the payment of the minimum subscribed share capital to at least 25% on initial allotment of shares, the whole of any premium must be paid up (eg if a company issues 50,000 £1 per shares at £1.50, the minimum subscribed share capital would be £37,500, ie one-quarter of £50,000 plus £25,000 premium) (s 101(2) and s 118).

A further distinction between the public and private company is now to be found in the company name. This was also an innovation in the Companies Act 1980. Thus a public company must end with the suffix 'public limited company' or the Welsh equivalent 'cwmni cyhoeddus cyfyngedig' or the abbreviation 'Plc' or 'ccc'. A private company should end with the word 'limited' or the Welsh equivalent 'cyfyngedig' or 'Ltd' or 'cyf' or, alternatively, 'unlimited' or 'anghyfyngedig'.

The fundamental distinction between the private and the public company is that the private company is prohibited from seeking finance from the public by offering its shares or debentures to the public. The public company by contrast may seek finance in this way.

The Companies Act and other pieces of legislation are peppered with a variety of other less important distinctions. Some of these are set out below:

- A private company need have only one director; a public company must have at least two.
- A private company need have only one member; a public company must have at least two.
- The company secretary of a public company must have a recognised professional qualification; there is no such requirement for a private company.
- Before a public company may pay a dividend, it must ensure not only that it has trading profits but also that its capital assets are maintained in value to at least the value of the subscribed share capital plus undistributable reserves. There is no such statutory rule imposing such a need on a private company.

- A public company before it may issue shares in exchange for property must obtain an independent expert's valuation of that property; there is no such need for a private company.
- A public company may not issue shares in exchange for services; there is no such restriction for a private company.
- A public company shall not allot shares in exchange for a consideration which includes an undertaking which may be performed more than five years after the date of allotment; there is no such restriction for a private company.
- The directors of a public company must call an extraordinary general meeting if it suffers a serious loss of capital; there is no such requirement placed upon the directors of a private company.
- Proxies in a private company may speak at the meeting; in public companies they may not.
- In a private company, there are certain courses of action that may be undertaken by elective resolution to dispense with certain formalities such as the holding of an annual general meeting, the laying of accounts and the annual appointment of auditors; there is no such provision for public companies.
- Private companies may act by unanimous written resolution in most cases; there is no such formal provision for public companies.
- Where it is proposed to elect a director aged 70 or above or to re-elect him to the board of a public company, special notice is required (this is also true of private companies which are subsidiaries of public companies); in relation to most private companies, there is no such requirement.

There are other distinctions between private and public companies but these represent some of the more well-known differences.

Corporate personality

It is commonplace in examinations for there to be a question on the principle of separate legal personality of the company or SLP as it is usually called in Malaysia where this chapter is being written. Sometimes these questions take the form of an essay. The principle was established in the landmark case of *Salomon v A Salomon & Co Ltd* (1897). The facts of this case were that Salomon had incorporated his boot and shoe repair business, transferring it to a company. He took all the shares of the company except six which were held by his wife, daughter and four sons. Part of the payment for the transfer of the business was made in the form of debentures (a secured loan) issued by the company to Salomon. Salomon transferred the debentures to Broderib in exchange for a loan. Salomon defaulted on payment of interest on the loan and Broderib sought to enforce the security against the company. Unsecured creditors tried to put the company into liquidation. A dispute ensued as to whether Broderib or the unsecured creditors had priority in relation to payment of the debts. It was argued for the unsecured creditors that Salomon's security was void as the company was a sham and was in reality the agent of Salomon. The House of Lords held that this was not the case and the company had been properly incorporated and that therefore the security was valid and could be enforced. The case is the most important case in company law since it is from this case that many of the principles of British company law flow. However, it has not been universally followed and there are exceptions to the *Salomon* principle where the corporate veil is lifted. Before turning to the exceptions, it is worth noting some applications of this basic principle. In *Lee v Lees Air Farming Ltd* (1961), a Privy Council case from New Zealand, Mrs Lee was widow of Mr Lee, who owned all of the shares except one and who was killed on company business flying the company's plane. Mrs Lee was able to argue that her husband was an employee and thus secured a pension from the New Zealand Workman's Compensation Fund. The *Salomon* principle was thus applied. In *Macaura v Northern Insurance Company Ltd* (1925), similarly, such an argument prevailed. Here, however, it was not in the interest of the shareholder concerned that the argument did succeed. The majority shareholder had continued to insure the timber that was destroyed by fire in his own name. The insurance company argued successfully that it was not his timber but that of the company (a relevant factor in the mind of the judge might well have been that the insurance was taken out shortly before the fire!). In *Gramophone & Typewriter Ltd v Stanley* (1908), the court held that the business of the company was not the business of the members. In *Tunstall v Steigmann* (1962), the plaintiff had transferred her butcher's business to a company. Above the shop there lived a tenant. Under the relevant provisions of the Landlord and Tenant Act 1954, the landlord is able to refuse a renewal of a tenancy if the premises are needed for the purposes of the business. This is what the plaintiff tried to do. The defendant argued successfully that the business no longer belonged to the plaintiff and so was outside the section. Such situations could not now arise because s 6 of the Law of Property Act 1969 provides that where a person has a controlling interest in a company which carries on the business, that person is able to treat the business as his own.

In *Lonrho Ltd v Shell Petroleum Company Ltd* (1980), we have another example of the application of the *Salomon* principle. In this case, Lonrho sought discovery of documents held by a subsidiary of Shell Petroleum in Southern Africa. The House of Lords held that the order for discovery did not extend to the subsidiary since this was a separate company.

More recently, in *Adams v Cape Industries Plc* (1990), there has been a restatement of the basic *Salomon* principle. It was noted by the Court of Appeal in that case *per* Slade LJ p 536:

... saving cases which turn on the wording of particular statutes or contracts, the court is not free to disregard the principle of *Salomon v A Salomon & Company Ltd* (1897) merely because it considers that justice so requires.

In tackling a question on the area of corporate personality, care should be taken to ensure that the answer that is drafted and prepared corresponds with the question that is asked. Sometimes the question will ask merely for a discussion about the statutory exceptions to the *Salomon* principle, eg 'Often parliament has intervened to mitigate the effect of the *Salomon* principle. Discuss'. On other occasions the question will be phrased in such a way that both statutory and judicial exceptions should be discussed, eg 'On occasion the courts and Parliament have intervened to mitigate the effects of the *Salomon* doctrine. Discuss'.

Statutory exceptions

There are various statutory exceptions:
* Section 24 of the Companies Act 1985 provides that if the membership of a company falls below the statutory minimum for a public company (two), then the remaining member should after a period of six months' grace be liable for the company's debts and obligations where he or she knows of the situation.
* Section 117(8) of the Companies Act 1985 provides that where a public company fails to obtain a trading certificate in addition to its certificate of incorporation before trading and borrowing money, then the company's directors are liable for any obligations incurred.
* Sections 226–31 of the Companies Act 1985 provide that where a group situation exists (ie where there is a holding company and subsidiaries), then group accounts should be prepared. In assessing whether this is the case, clearly the veil is being lifted to determine

if the holding company/subsidiary company relationship exists (see the definition of holding and subsidiary companies in s 736, s 736A and s 736B of the Companies Act 1985).

- Section 349(4) of the Companies Act 1985 provides that if a company officer misdescribes the company in a letter, bill, invoice, order, receipt or other document, then the officer is liable in the event of the company not honouring the obligation concerned. The section is strict and would cover any abbreviation or misdescription except abbreviations such as 'Ltd', 'cyf', 'Plc', 'ccc' or 'co'.

- Section 459 of the Companies Act 1985 may involve lifting the veil to determine, for example, the basis on which the company was formed (see *Re London School of Electronics* (1986)).

- Sections 736–36B of the Companies Act 1985 set out the formula for determining if a holding company/subsidiary company relationship exists.

- Section 15 of the Company Directors' Disqualification Act 1986 provides that if a director who is disqualified continues to act, then he will be personally liable for the debts and obligations of the company.

- Section 122(1)(g) of the Insolvency Act 1986 provides that a petitioner may present a petition to wind the company up on the just and equitable ground. On occasion this may be based on a situation involving lifting of the veil, as in *Ebrahimi v Westbourne Galleries* (1973) where the petitioner was pointing to the basis on which the company had been formed.

- Section 213 of the Insolvency Act 1986 provides that where a person trades through the medium of a company knowing that the company is unable to pay its debts as they fall due, he or she may be held liable to make contributions to the company's assets. This has a criminal counterpart in s 458 of the Companies Act 1985.

- Section 214 of the Insolvency Act 1986 provides that where a director or shadow director ought to know that the company is unable to pay its debts as they fall due, he may be held liable to make a contribution to the company's assets where the company is being wound up.

- Section 6 of the Law of Property Act 1969 which has been referred to above (p 6) alters the effect of *Tunstall v Steigmann* by providing that where a person has a controlling interest in a company which is carrying on a business, the business is treated as the controller for the purposes of refusing a renewal of a tenancy under the Landlord and Tenant Act 1954.

Judicial exceptions

In addition to the statutory exceptions to the *Salomon* principle there are also judicial decisions where the veil is lifted.

It is not easy to categorise these cases but there are some consistent themes which can be singled out. One of these is to combat fraud.

Combatting fraud

In *Jones v Lipman* (1962) a vendor had agreed to sell a piece of land. Subsequently, he changed his mind. In an effort to defeat a move to obtain specific performance the vendor transferred the land to a company which he controlled. The court refused to countenance this. The veil was lifted and specific performance was ordered against the vendor and the company.

In *Gilford Motor Co v Horne* (1933) an employee had entered into an agreement not to compete with his former employer after ceasing employment. In order to try to avoid this restriction the employee set up a company and acted through that. The court held that this manoeuvre would not be tolerated, the veil would be lifted and an injunction would be issued against the company too.

There are other examples of the veil being lifted to combat fraud:

- *Re Darby ex p Brougham* (1911)
- *Re FG (Films) Ltd* (1953)
- *Re Bugle Press* (1961)
- *Wallersteiner v Moir* (1974).

Another theme which runs through the cases is agency. Often the veil will be lifted where an agency is found to exist.

Agency

In *Salomon* itself agency had been rejected by the House of Lords.

In *Smith, Stone and Knight Ltd v Birmingham Corporation* (1939) Atkinson J lifted the veil to enable a subsidiary company operating business on land owned by the holding company to claim compensation on the ground of agency.

In *Firestone Tyre and Rubber Co Ltd v Lewellin* (1957) agency was once again the trigger for lifting the veil where a British company manufacturing tyres for an American holding company was held to be its agent. In *Re FG (Films) Ltd* (1953) where fraud or sharp practice was also a factor, the American holding company set up a British subsidiary to produce the film 'Monsoon'. It was held that there was an agency and that the film was an American one.

Groups

Sometimes the fact that a company is within a group is seen as a reason for identifying it with another company within the group in addition to the statutory situations where the veil is lifted on this basis.

In *Harold Holdsworth & Co (Wakefield) Ltd v Caddies* (1955) the respondent held an employment contract with the appellant company to serve it as Managing Director. The House of Lords held that the appellant company could require the respondent to serve a subsidiary company.

The case that is widely seen as the leading case in this area although it is only a Court of Appeal decision is *DHN Food Distributors Ltd v Tower Hamlets London Borough Council* (1976). Like *Smith, Stone and Knight Ltd v Birmingham Corporation* the case concerned compensation for compulsory purchase. Here the company operating the business was the holding company and the premises were owned by the company's wholly owned subsidiary. Like *Smith, Stone and Knight Ltd* compensation was only payable for disturbance of the business if the business was operated on land owned by the company.

Lord Denning MR said:

... we all know that in many respects a group of companies are treated together for the purpose of general accounts, balance sheet and profit and loss account. They are treated as one concern ... This is especially the case when a parent company owns all the shares of the subsidiary – so much so that it can control every movement of the subsidiaries. These subsidiaries are bound hand and foot and must do just what the parent company says.

However, it is not every wholly owned subsidiary that is identified with its holding company. It did not happen, for example, in *Lonrho Ltd v Shell Petroleum Co Ltd* (1980). (See also *Woolfson and Another v Strathclyde Regional Council* (1978).)

Trust

The concept of the trust has also been utilised on occasion to circumvent the corporate facade. In *Trebanog Working Men's Club and Institute Ltd v Macdonald* (1940) the club was charged with selling liquor without a licence. It was held by the divisional court that the club in fact held the liquor on trust for its members so there was no offence.

In *The Abbey, Malvern Wells Ltd v Ministry of Local Government and Planning* (1951) it was held that shares in a company were held on trusts and that those directing the affairs of the company were trustees so that the court could lift the veil and impose the terms of the trust on the company's property.

Conclusions

This is a favourite examination topic. It is a straightforward area and although there is no magic categorisation of the judicial exceptions it is likely that the categorisation set out here will be helpful. Try to read up on this area, delve into some of the cases. Spice your answers up with academic citation from other sources. Above all else be sure to read the examination question carefully and tailor your answer accordingly – many a strong candidate has 'come a cropper' answering a question that has not been set!

Companies – crimes and torts

It is accepted that companies can commit crimes. There are certain exceptions by their very nature. Companies cannot commit crimes such as rape, incest etc. Also companies cannot commit crimes where there is a mandatory sentence of imprisonment, such as murder. It seems to be accepted though that companies may commit manslaughter, see the Zeebrugge Ferry disaster, *R v HM Coroner for East Kent ex p Spooner and others* (1987).

In December 1994, OLL Limited became the first company in England to be convicted of manslaughter. This arose from the deaths of four teenagers in a canoeing disaster in Lyme Bay whilst on a trip organised by the company.

In *Kite v OLL Ltd*, the Managing Director of the company that had organised the trip was imprisoned for manslaughter and the company was fined a total of £60,000.

The Law Commission consulted on the law of corporate manslaughter in Consultation Paper No 135 (1994). The Law Commission recommended a new offence based on whether the company's conduct fell significantly below what could reasonably be expected of it in the context of the significant risk of death or injury of which it should have been aware.

In a later report (Law Commission Paper No 237), Legislating the Criminal Code; Involuntary Manslaughter (1996), the Law Commission, in its final report, calls for a new offence of corporate killing comparable to killing by gross negligence. The report backs away from recommending jail sentences for directors of convicted companies, however.

It seems imperative that at least one person has to be identified as the directing mind of the company causing death by gross negligence when acting as the company. In the only other case of a company being convicted of manslaughter, Jackson Transport (Ossett) Ltd, the company concerned was a medium-sized company, employing about 40 people. James Hodgson was killed in May 1994 while he was cleaning behind a tanker vehicle containing chemicals.

The decision is of importance because the company was not a small one like OLL Ltd, although Jackson, as Managing Director, did run the business himself. Jackson and the company were both convicted of manslaughter in September 1996.

In *Tesco v Nattrass* (1992), the principle of identification was established. This means that the state of the directing mind and will of the company can be attributed to the company. In *Tesco Supermarket Ltd v Nattrass* (1992), the company was charged with an offence under the Trade Descriptions Act 1968, when it stated that goods available were available at sale price when they were not. The company demonstrated that it had introduced a system to try to ensure that this did not happen. The failure was that of the Store Manager and not of the company and for this the company was held not liable.

Shortcomings in the identification approach were recognised in the Privy Council case of *Meridian Global Fund Management Asia Ltd v The Securities Commission* (1995). The Privy Council held that in certain cases the court had to determine whose act or knowledge was the company's. Generally this would be the directing mind and will of the company, but not necessarily so.

Meridian was unusual in that a company was convicted of a crime where the individual whose knowledge was attributed to the company, was not part of the company's directing mind and will. As Lord Hoffmann said in the case, 'whose acts (knowledge or state of mind) was for this purpose intended to count as the acts etc of the company? One finds the answer to this question by applying the usual cannons of interpretation, taking into account the language of the rule (if it is a statute) and its contents and policy'.

The policy of the New Zealand Securities Amendment Act 1988, which was at issue in *Meridian*, was to require the immediate disclosure of a substantial security holder. The person here, whose knowledge was attributed to the company, was the person who acquired the relevant interest with the company's authority.

Three cases in the 1940s had established that companies could commit crimes involving dishonesty: *DPP v Kent and Sussex Contractors Ltd* (1944), *R v ICR Haulage Ltd* (1944) and *Moore v Bresler Ltd* (1944).

Companies may also clearly commit strict liability offences. This is important in areas such as pollution and food safety. However, there is a diligence defence and if the company can demonstrate the practice of diligence, or that the lack of diligence was on the part of the person who was not the true embodiment of the company, it will then escape liability.

Companies may also commit torts. Not only will a company be liable for the torts of employees committed in the course of their employment on the basis of careless liability, but they may also be liable in their own right. Thus the company may be liable for nuisance etc.

2 The company's constitution

You should be familiar with the following areas:

- the contents of the company's memorandum of association
- the methods of changing the various clauses of the company's memorandum of association
- the company's objects clause and the *ultra vires* doctrine
- the contents of the company's articles of association
- the method for changing the articles of association and restrictions on changes
- the variation of class rights
- the membership contract

Introduction

It is proposed to look at certain areas in depth, exploring those that are considered to be essential such as objects clauses, and a company's articles. Other areas are dealt with in less depth.

The contents of the company's memorandum

The memorandum of association or memorandum (as it is generally known), is sometimes termed the external constitution of the company. This document sets out certain key features of the company's status. The memorandum must contain the following:

- the name of the company (s 2(1)(a));
- a statement that the company is a public company if that is the case (s 1(3));

- a statement that the registered office of the company is to be situated in England and Wales, in Wales or in Scotland (s 2(1)(b));
- the objects of the company (s 2(1)(3));
- if the company is limited by guarantee or by share capital a statement to that effect (s 2(3));
- if the company has a share capital, the memorandum must state the amount of the share capital and the division of the share capital into shares of a fixed amount (s 2(5));
- the memorandum may contain additional clauses (s 17), these may be altered by special resolution, but a dissentient minority of 15% may seek to stop the alteration.

Alterations to the memorandum

The statutory provisions of the Companies Act 1985 governing changes to the relevant part of the memorandum are set out below:
- generally (s 2(7));
- change of name (s 28);
- change from public status to private (ss 53–55);
- change from private status to public (ss 43–48);
- change of objects (ss 4–5);
- change from limited status to unlimited (ss 49–50);
- change from unlimited status to limited (ss 51–52);
- changes of share capital
   (a) increase (s 121(2)(a)),
   (b) cancellation of unissued shares (s 121(2)(e)),
   (c) reduction of issued shares (ss 135–38);
- change of other matters contained in the memorandum (s 17).

Objects clauses and *ultra vires*

Despite or perhaps because of the changes made to the law on *ultra vires* by the Companies Act 1989, this area remains a favourite examination topic.

A company still needs to have an objects clause and care should be taken in drafting the clause as fatal consequences could flow from a poorly drafted objects clause.

Since the Companies Act 1989, what is now s 3A, permits a company to opt for a general commercial objects clause. Where the company's memorandum states that the object of the company is to carry on business as a general commercial company:

- the object of the company is to carry on any trade or business whatsoever; and
- the company has power to do all such things as are incidental or conducive to the carrying on of any trade or business by it.

Such a clause should cover any activity that a trading company is likely to wish to engage in and therefore few problems should arise. For this same reason general objects clauses are not beloved of examiners. Problems are far more likely to involve restrictive objects clauses.

If a company has as its one and only object, for example, 'The organising of foreign holidays in the Aegean', if the directors propose that the company should start to manufacture motor cars, a shareholder will be able to obtain an injunction to restrain this (s 35(2) of the Companies Act 1985). Such a move is only possible, however, as a pre-emptory strike before the company has entered into a transaction – no later.

Drafting devices

Sometimes particular words or phrases may have the effect of extending the company's room for manoeuvre:

- If there is a provision that states that all of the company's objects are main and independent, then no object can be interpreted as subsidiary to another or given effect only in relation to that other object. In *Cotman v Brougham* (1918) there was a main and independent objects sub-clause:

... every sub-clause is to be construed as a substantive clause and is not to be limited or restricted by reference to any other sub-clause or by the name of the company, and no sub-clause nor the object specified therein is to be deemed subsidiary or auxiliary merely to the objects mentioned in the first sub-clause.

This was held to be effective to render all of the activities set out in earlier sub-clauses *intra vires* and render valid the underwriting of shares in an oil company by a company whose main economic activity was the production of rubber.

- There may be a rounding off clause which has the effect of giving the directors extended power to act. This is what was at issue in *Bell*

Houses Ltd v City Wall Properties (1966) where there was a rounding off clause which provided that the company could:

... carry on any other trade or business whatsoever which can in the opinion of the board of directors be advantageously carried on by the company in connection with or as ancillary to any of the above businesses or the general business of the company.

- The use of generic words can make the drafting of objects clauses simpler and crisper, eg the use of the word 'merchants' in *Re New Finance & Mortgage Co* (1975).
- In *Newstead v Frost* (1980) the issue was whether the objects clause of the company allowed the company to carry on business in partnership with David Frost to exploit copyrights and to act as consultants, advisors and publicity agents throughout the world outside the UK. The House of Lords held that the objects clause in the memorandum did cover the activities. Viscount Dilhorne quoted the relevant provision in the objects clause as follows:

... Clause 3 of the memorandum sets out the objects of the company and Clause 3(6) reads as follows: to carry on business as bankers, capitalists, financiers, concessionaires and merchants and to undertake and carry on and execute all kinds of financial commercial trading or other operations and generally to undertake and carry out all such transactions as an individual capitalist may lawfully undertake and carry out.

The paragraph ends with the following statement:

And it is hereby declared that the objects of the company specified in each of the foregoing paragraphs of this clause ... shall be separate and distinct objects of the company and shall not be in any ways limited by reference to any other paragraph or the order in which the same occur or by the name of the company.

In holding this objects clause a valid statement of objects the House of Lords is clearly indicating that companies can opt for general objects clauses which will cover most trading activities. Such a decision coupled with other decisions on interpretation of the objects clause underlined the limitations of the existing *ultra vires* doctrine. The whole basis of the doctrine has increasingly been questioned.

The position at common law

At common law contracts that were outside the scope of the company's objects clause were *ultra vires* and void. Before statutory intervention, therefore, the question was relatively simple. If the objects clause covered the relevant contract it was valid, if it was outside of the company's permitted range of activities it was void. The whole doctrine rested on the principle of constructive notice, the rule in *Ernest v Nicholls* (1857), whereby a person dealing with a company was deemed to know the contents of the company's memorandum of association and articles of association.

On occasion the question might be slightly more problematic. Whilst a person dealing with a company was entitled to assume that where an activity could have been executed in an *ultra vires* or in an *intra vires* way that it would be carried out in an *intra vires* way sometimes the other party would be put on notice of the *ultra vires* nature of the activity. This can be illustrated by comparing two cases. In *Re Payne (David) & Co Ltd* (1904) where a company borrowed money which was in fact used for *ultra vires* business the lender of the money was able to enforce the loan since he did not know the purpose of the loan. In *Re John Beauforte (London) Ltd* (1953) a different decision was reached. A supplier provided a company with coke. In fact the coke could have been used for the *intra vires* business of the company manufacturing dresses and robes. The company was actually in the business of manufacturing veneered panels. Since the order was placed on notepaper showing that the company was engaged in this business the court held that the combination of constructive notice of what the company could do and actual notice of what it was doing was fatal to the supplier's claim.

Fine distinctions were once made between matters that are set out in the objects clause in the nature of powers and objects properly so called. In *Re Introductions Ltd* (1970) the company borrowed money from the National Westminster Bank. The money was in fact used for the *ultra vires* business of financing pig breeding. The lender sought to rely on the provision in the objects clause allowing the company to borrow money. It was held that borrowing was not capable of standing as a substantive object and therefore the lender must fail. In *Rolled Steel Products (Holdings) Ltd v British Steel Corporation and others* (1986) the law was reviewed. The objects of the plaintiff company included the capacity to:

... lend or advance money or give credit to such persons, firms or companies on such terms as may seem expedient and to give guarantees or become security for any such persons, firms or companies.

In this case there was a complex web of transactions between the plaintiff, the defendant and a third company. It was argued that the giving of a guarantee and a debenture to secure the guarantee were both void in this case. The Court of Appeal, however, held that the giving of the guarantee and the debenture to secure it were within the capacity of the company.

Slade LJ in the Court of Appeal considered that the basic rule is that a company incorporated under the Companies Acts has capacity to do those acts falling within the objects set out in the memorandum of association or such activities as are reasonably incidental to the attainment or pursuit of those objects. He went on to say that if a particular act such as the giving of the guarantee and the securing of it by the debenture in the instant case is of a category which on construction of the company's memorandum is capable of being performed as reasonably incidental to the attainment or the pursuit of the objects it is not rendered *ultra vires* merely because in a particular instance the directors in performing the act in the name of the company are actually doing so for purposes other than those set out in the memorandum.

The decision in *Rolled Steel Products v British Steel Corporation* therefore put another nail in the coffin of the doctrine of *ultra vires* as once again it provided extra latitude to the company and its directors acting in its name. (It is worth noting that the relevant facts in *Rolled Steel* occurred before the European Communities Act 1972 came into force although the decision was only reported in 1986.)

Statutory intervention

When the UK acceded to the European Communities in 1972 the first directive on company law had already been passed. Article 9 of the first EC directive on company law provided as follows:

- Acts done by the organs of the company shall be binding upon it even if those acts are not within the objects of the company, unless such acts exceed powers that the law confers or allows to be conferred on those organs.

However, Member States may provide that the company shall not be bound where such acts are outside the objects of the company, if it proves that the third party knew the act was outside those objects or could not in view of the circumstances have been unaware of it; disclosure of the statute shall not in itself be sufficient proof thereof.

- The limits on the powers of the organs of the company, arising under the statutes from the decision of the competent organ, may never be relied on as against third parties, even if they have been disclosed.

Accordingly when the UK joined the European Communities the European Communities Act 1972 provided in s 9(1):

In favour of a person dealing with a company in good faith any transaction decided on by the directors shall be deemed to be one which it is within the capacity of the company to enter into and the power of the directors to bind the company shall be deemed to be free of any limitation under the memorandum or articles of association, and a party to a transaction so decided on shall not be bound to enquire as to the capacity of the company to enter into it or as to any such limitation on the power of the directors, and shall be presumed to have acted in good faith unless the contrary is proved.

Examination questions used to focus on the application of s 9(1) of the European Communities Act 1972 and difficulties with its interpretation. This section has now been superseded by the reforms of the Companies Act 1989 but background information on the pitfalls and difficulties of the old section are instructive and help to explain how the law has developed.

Section 9(1) of the European Communities Act 1972 only operated in favour of a person dealing with the company. The company itself could not take advantage of the section.

The section only operated where the person dealing with the company was acting in good faith.

No definition of good faith was contained in this section but there was a presumption of good faith that stands unless the contrary is proved. In *Barclays Bank Ltd v TOSG Trust Fund Ltd* (1984) Nourse J stated *obiter* that a person acts in good faith if he acts genuinely and honestly in the circumstances of the case and that it is not necessary to show that he acted reasonably to demonstrate that he acted in good faith.

The transaction had to be decided on by the directors. The section gave no guidance as to how this was to be assessed. It seems from the decision in *International Sales and Agencies v Marcus* (1982) that if a chain of delegation can be traced back to the board of directors then the transaction had indeed been decided on by the directors.

The wording of the section clearly indicated that the law only covered the area of contract. The use of the word 'dealing' in particular denotes a contractual arrangement. The section, therefore, had no scope beyond the law of contract. This reform clearly mitigated the law of *ultra vires* by allowing the other party to the transaction with a

21

company to enforce the transaction in many circumstances. The position was still far from satisfactory however. Companies could avoid the *ultra vires* trap by widely drawn objects clauses and where the *ultra vires* doctrine did operate it was a matter of caprice and chance catching the unwary. The government asked Dr Dan Prentice of Oxford University to consider reform of the *ultra vires* rule. This report was published as a consultative document, 'Reform of the *Ultra Vires* Rule: a Consultative Document' (1986). Dr Prentice proposed in para 50 that:

- a company should have the capacity to do any act whatsoever;
- a third party dealing with the company should not be affected by the contents of any document merely because it is registered with the registrar of companies or with the company (this could be made subject to appropriate exceptions);
- a company should be bound by the acts of its board or of an individual director;
- the third party should be under no obligation to determine the scope of the authority of a company's board or individual director, or the contents of the company's articles or memorandum (this should extend to documents which have to be registered under s 380 of the Companies Act 1985);
- the third party who has actual knowledge that a board or an individual director do not possess the authority to enter into a transaction on behalf of the company should not be allowed to enforce it against the company but the company should be free to ratify this. The same result should obtain where a third party has actual knowledge that the transaction falls outside the company's objects but in this case ratification should be by a special resolution;
- knowledge in this context will require understanding and it will only be the knowledge of the individual entering into the particular transaction which will be relevant;
- the proposal (in relation to third parties) should be modified where a third party is an officer or a director of the company and in this situation constructive knowledge should be sufficient to render the transaction unenforceable and for this purpose constructive knowledge should mean the type of knowledge which may reasonably be expected of a person carrying out the functions of that director or officer of that company.

In reaching these conclusions Dr Prentice had considered that in para 11:

... the doctrine of *ultra vires* has failed to provide any significant protection to either creditors or shareholders. In so far as either creditors or shareholders have a legitimate interest in ensuring that the company restricts its activities to those enumerated in its objects clause, this can be achieved in other ways. To provide such protection it is not necessary to impose restrictions on a company's capacity which could prejudice the third party dealing with the company.

In consequence of Dr Prentice's recommendations the Companies Act 1989 amended the law on *ultra vires* and objects clauses.

It is first worth noting that the law was altered in relation to objects clauses. Mention has already been made above of the new s 3A permitting a company to opt for a general commercial objects clause. At the same time the law was amended to allow a company to change its objects by special resolution without restriction. Previously only certain alterations of objects within the permitted heads set out in the old s 4 were permitted.

The 1989 Act and a company's capacity

Henceforth s 35(1) of the Companies Act 1985 provides that the validity of an act done by a company shall not be called into question on the ground of lack of capacity by reason of anything in the company's memorandum. A transaction can thus be enforced by an outsider or by the company.

A member may, however, restrain the company from entering into a transaction which is outside the companies objects. Section 35(2) of the Companies Act 1985 permits this before the transaction has been concluded. The law here has not changed see *Simpson v Westminster Palace Hotel Company* (1860), *Stephens v Mysore Reefs (Kangundy) Mining Company* (1902). This power to restrain the company, however, can only operate when the company has not entered into a binding transaction to perform an act.

If the directors exceed limitations on their powers then they are in breach of their directors' duties. Therefore, even if the directors conclude a contract outside the scope of the objects clause, and a member has not succeeded in restraining this, the company may be able to sue the directors for breach of their duties (see s 35(3) of the Companies Act 1985). It is open to the company to ratify what has been done by special resolution. The company may also ratify by a separate special resolution the breach of directors' duties thus putting the matter beyond litigation.

Section 35A now provides that where a person deals with a company in good faith the power of the directors to bind the company shall be deemed to be free of any limitation under the company's constitution. The outsider is not to be regarded as in bad faith by reason only of his knowing that the transaction was beyond the directors' powers.

Section 35A protects an outsider who deals with the company and 'deals' is now defined as where a person is a party to any transaction or other act. This is clearly broader than the old law outlined above. It seems to include the receipt of cheques (see *International Sales and Agencies Ltd v Marcus* under the old law).

Section 35B of the Act goes on to provide:

> ... a party to a transaction with a company is not bound to enquire as to whether it is permitted by the company's memorandum or as to any limitation on the powers of the board of directors to bind the company or authorise others to do so.

The wording of ss 35A and 35B will protect outsiders in most circumstances and clearly abolishes constructive notice in relation to directors in such circumstances. The provisions are added to by s 711A which would extend to other officers acting on behalf of the company. Section 711A(1) provides that:

> ... a person shall not be taken to have notice of any matter merely because of its being disclosed in any document kept by the registrar of companies (and thus available for inspection) or made available by the company for inspection.

Section 711A(2) provides:

> ... this does not affect the question whether a person is affected by notice of any matter by reason of a failure to make such enquiries as ought reasonably to be made.

Section 711A(2) does introduce an element of doubt relating to the abolition of the doctrine. It is a moot point as to the circumstances where a person is put on notice and should make enquiries relating to a matter.

Dr Prentice had recommended a special provision to deal with transactions entered into by the company with a person who is a director or a person connected with a director. Section 322A provided that a transaction is voidable if it exceeds a limitation of the powers of the board of directors under the company's constitution if one of the parties to the transaction included:

- a director of the company or of its holding company; or
- a person connected with such a director or a company with whom such a director is associated, at the option of the company.

Special provision is also made in relation to charities. Dr Prentice noted in his report 'that it is an overriding requirement of public policy that a charitable company may devote its assets to the purposes set out in the company's objects and that it should not use its assets for other purposes so as to frustrate the entitlements of the beneficiaries of the company's charitable purposes, or to break faith with any donors'. Dr Prentice, however, had come down against treating charities differently. In the event the law does still make a distinction. Section 65 of the Charities Act 1993 deals with the position. The Companies Act 1989 reforms in relation to *ultra vires* do not apply to a company which is a charity except in favour of a person who gives full consideration in money or money's worth and does not know that the act is beyond the company's objects clause or beyond the directors' powers or who does not know at the time that the act is done that the company is a charity.

Ultra vires and objects clauses remain favourite examination areas. The ground has shifted, however. You should make sure that you are familiar with the Prentice Report recommendations, with the Companies Act 1989 and the history behind the changes. Ensure that you are familiar with the way in which *ultra vires* remains important:

- to restrain a company which is proposing to act beyond its objects;
- to bring directors to account for breach of directors' duties;
- in relation to directors dealing with their companies or with subsidiaries of their holding companies;
- in relation to charitable companies.

Company name

Some knowledge of the rules governing the choice of name for a company is helpful. Although it is rare for there to be a specific question on the company name it may feature as part of a problem question.

The first clause in the company's memorandum should set out the company's name. The statutory provisions relating to company names are set out in ss 25–34 of the Companies Act 1985. These provisions provide as follows:

- Section 25 of the Act provides that the name of a public company must end with the words public limited company or the recognised abbreviation 'Plc' or the Welsh equivalent 'cwmni cyhoeddus cyfyngedig' or 'ccc'. By contrast a private company limited by shares or by guarantee should end with 'limited' or the recognised

25

abbreviation 'Ltd' or the Welsh equivalent 'cyfyngedig' or 'cyf'. Sometimes a private limited company may be permitted to omit the word limited from the end of its name. Previously, this was the case under the Companies Act 1948 where companies could obtain a licence, if their work was for charity or public good, to omit the word limited. Section 30 of the Companies Act 1985 now permits companies to omit the word limited on satisfying certain conditions. The company concerned must be a private limited company and have as its objects the promotion of commerce, art, science, education, religion, charity or any profession, and anything incidental or conducive to any of those objects and must have a requirement in its constitution that its profits or other income be applied in promoting those objects. The constitution must also prohibit the payment of dividends to its members and require all of the assets which would otherwise be available to its members generally to be transferred on its winding up to another body with similar objects or to a body the objects of which are the promotion of charity and anything incidental or conducive thereto. Where such an exemption from using the word limited is desired then a statutory declaration that a company complies with the above requirements must be delivered to the registrar of companies who may accept the declaration as evidence of the matters stated in it. The registrar may refuse to register a company by a name which does not include the word limited unless such a declaration has been delivered to him (if the company is limited).

- Section 26 of the Companies Act 1985 prohibits the use of certain names. The words public limited company, limited and unlimited can only be used at the end of the company name as may the Welsh equivalents cwmni cyhoeddus cyfyngedig, cyfyngedig and anghyfyngedig respectively. The same principle applies to the recognised abbreviations of these words or expressions. Names which would in the opinion of the Secretary of State constitute a criminal offence or which in the opinion of the Secretary of State would be offensive are also forbidden. Certain words may only be used with the approval of the Secretary of State. Thus, if the name in the opinion of the Secretary of State would be likely to give the impression that the company is connected with Her Majesty's government or a local authority then approval is needed (s 26(2)(a) of the Companies Act 1985).

- The name must not be the same as a name already appearing on the index of company names kept by the registrar of companies under s 714 of the Companies Act 1985 (s 26(2)(b) of the Companies Act

1985). For the purposes of deciding whether a name is the same as one already on the register, certain matters are ignored. These matters are:

(a) the occurrence of the definite article in the beginning of the name;

(b) the occurrence of the words 'company', 'limited' or 'unlimited' or 'public limited company' or any abbreviated or Welsh form of these words.

(c) the topography, word division, accenting or punctuation of the name. If a name should be registered by the registrar and it is subsequently discovered that the name is the same as an existing name or too like an existing name or a name that should have appeared on the index at that time then the Secretary of State can within 12 months of the registration require the company to change its name (s 28(2) of the Companies Act 1985).

• There are certain words and expressions which require the prior permission of either the Secretary of State or some other designated body (s 29 of the Companies Act 1985). There is a list of the words specified in regulations made under s 29 of the Companies Act. If the name of the company implies some regional, national or international pre-eminence, governmental link or sponsorship or some pre-eminent status, then consent may well be required. Thus, if it is desired to use the word 'University' the consent of the Privy Council would be needed. In seeking registration of the company name it would be appropriate to have copies of the letters sent to the relevant body and the response indicating that there is no objection when seeking registration with that name.

• The choice of company name is limited by other considerations. If the name constitutes a registered trademark the person who has the trademark may institute summary proceedings to prevent the use of the name under the Trade Marks Act 1994.

• The use of the name which is already used by an existing business (whether sole trader, partnership or company) or a name which is similar to that of an existing business such as it appears to the trading public that there is a link between the two businesses may be subject to a passing off action in tort which if successful will involve the granting of an injunction to prevent further use of the name and an account of profits in respect of the past use of the name. Thus, in *Ewing v Buttercup Margarine Ltd* (1917) Astbury J, affirmed by the Court of Appeal, held that the plaintiff who operated the Buttercup Dairy Company could obtain an injunction against the Buttercup Margarine Company since this name was calculated to deceive by diverting customers, or potential customers, from the plaintiff to the defendant. Less obviously, in *Chill Foods (Scotland) Ltd v Cool Foods Ltd* (1977) Murray and Dick had run a company called S & J Catering Products Ltd (S & J) which acquired a company called Chill Foods (Scotland) Ltd (Chill Foods). Dick then founded a company called Cool Foods Ltd trading in the same areas as S & J and Chill Foods. An interdict was granted preventing Cool Foods Ltd trading because of the similarity of name, similarity of business and the similarity of trading areas. It is not automatic that an injunction will be granted even where a business has an identical name. There must clearly be some similarity in the trading area and the business concern. Thus in *Tussaud v Tussaud* (1890), Madame Tussaud and Sons Ltd were granted an injunction to restrain Louis Tussaud Ltd from carrying on a similar business, namely a waxworks exhibition in Shaftesbury Avenue, which was clearly similar to the one 'so long and successfully carried on in Baker Street and the Marylebone Road'.

* A novel, if unsuccessful argument, was deployed in *Exxon Corporation and Others v Exxon Insurance International Ltd* (1982) where the plaintiffs claimed copyright in the word 'Exxon' as an original literary work under s 2 of the Copyright Act 1956. The Court of Appeal held that the single word could not qualify as an original literary work so the defendant could not be restrained from using it on the grounds of breach of copyright.

Change of name

Section 28 of the Companies Act 1985 provides that a company may change its name by special resolution in general meeting. The same rules apply on a change of name as apply to the initial choice of name.

Sometimes the Secretary of State may require a change of name. It has already been noted that if he finds that the name is too similar to an existing name he may require a change within 12 months (s 28(2) of the Companies Act 1985). This applies in just the same way after a name has been changed as on a choice of name on initial incorporation.

If a company provides misleading information to the registrar on incorporation or on a change of a name the registrar may order a change within five years (s 28(3) of the Companies Act 1985).

The Secretary of State may also require an alteration of name if he believes that it gives a misleading indication of the nature or activities of the company so as to be likely to cause harm to the public. This power may be exercised at any time (s 32(1) of the Companies Act 1985). The direction must be complied with within six weeks.

Articles of association

Together with the memorandum of association, which is submitted to the registrar when the company is seeking incorporation, is the document entitled the articles of association. In practice, the two documents are attached together.

If the company is a company limited by guarantee or an unlimited company the articles must be printed, divided into paragraphs and numbered. In the case of a company limited by shares, if individual articles are not registered or if articles are registered which are incomplete then the relevant Table A will apply in full or part. There have been various sets of Table A articles. The current set is the Companies (Tables A–F) Regulations 1985 SI 1985/805. For a company registering today these would be the Table A articles that would apply. Companies that are already registered may have other Table A articles applying to them, eg Table A of the First Schedule of the Companies Act 1948. It is possible for such companies to update their articles and apply later Table A articles.

It is usual for a company to adopt Table A articles with modifications to its own particular circumstances.

In examination terms the areas that are most likely to be examinable in relation to articles of association are either the alteration of the articles and restrictions upon alterability or the membership contract (s 14 of the Companies Act 1985) which in fact governs the memorandum and articles of association although the provisions in the articles are more likely to impinge upon members.

Alteration of the articles

It is said that a company's articles are freely alterable. Section 9 of the Companies Act 1985 provides that a company may by special resolution alter its articles. A company may not be injuncted where it has agreed not to alter its articles (see *Punt v Symons & Co* (1903)). In fact this power to alter the articles of association of a company is subject to various restrictions.

- The company cannot alter its articles to contravene the provisions of the Companies Act. For example a provision in the articles which seeks to exempt an officer of the company from liability for negligence would be void by virtue of s 310 of the Companies Act 1985. In the same way a provision seeking to increase the liability of a member beyond that of his original contractual obligation is void by virtue of s 16 of the Companies Act 1985. Section 16(1) provides:

... a member of a company is not bound by an alteration made in the memorandum or articles after the date on which he became a member, if and so far as the alteration:

(a) requires him to take or subscribe for more shares than the number held by him at the date on which the alteration is made; or

(b) in anyway increases his liability as at that date to contribute to the company's share capital or otherwise to pay money to the company

Indeed s 9 itself provides that the power is subject to the provisions of the Act.

- Any alteration of the company's articles which clashes with a provision in the company's memorandum is void. Section 9 itself provides that the power is subject to the conditions contained in the company's memorandum. In *Guinness v The Land Corporation of Ireland* (1882) the company's objects included the cultivation of land in Ireland. The memorandum of association provided that share capital would be divided into A shares and B shares. Article 8 of the articles of association provided that the B share capital could be applied to pay a dividend of 5% per annum on the A shares if this were needed. Chitty J and the Court of Appeal upholding him held that this provision was invalid as it was at odds with the memorandum of association.

- If an alteration of the articles is proposed which conflicts with an order of the court then this is, of course, void. For example, an order of the court under s 5 of the Companies Act 1985 relating to a change of objects or under s 461 of the Companies Act 1985 relating to the remedy for unfairly prejudicial conduct cannot be overridden by a change of articles.

- If the proposed alteration of articles involves an alteration or abrogation of class rights then special procedures have to be followed in addition to the passing of a special resolution as required under s 9 of the Companies Act 1985. The company must follow the regime which is appropriate to the variation of class rights which is set out in ss 125–27 of the Companies Act 1985.

Clearly if the change of articles also involves a variation of class rights the procedure must be followed. If the company has more than one class of share then questions of variation of class rights sometimes arise. Generally, it will be obvious if there is more than one class of share. The shares will generally have a label attached to them, eg ordinary shares or preference shares. However, it is not always so simple. On occasion, if particular rights attach to a certain shareholding this might constitute those shares as a separate class of shares. This was held to be the position in *Cumbrian Newspapers Group Ltd v Cumberland and Westmorland Herald Newspaper and Printing Company Ltd* (1986).

In that case the plaintiff company, Cumbrian Newspapers Ltd was the holder of 10.67% of the issued ordinary shares of the defendant company, Cumberland and Westmorland Herald Newspaper and Printing Company Ltd. The defendant company's articles provided, *inter alia*, for a right of pre-emption over any shares which are being transferred in favour of the plaintiff. Furthermore, Article 12 in the articles of association provided that:

... if and so long as Cumberland Newspapers Ltd should be registered as the holder of not less than one tenth in nominal value of the issued ordinary share capital of the company Cumberland Newspapers Ltd shall be entitled from time to time to nominate one person to be a director of the company.

Scott J held that the shares held by Cumbrian Newspapers Group constituted a separate class of shares.

Once it has been determined that there is more than one class of share in the company the next question for determination is whether there has been a variation of the rights attaching to those shares. Once again this may not be as straightforward as it at first appears. By contrast with the question of whether there is more than one class of share the approach of the courts here is somewhat restrictive. The question had to be considered, for example, in *Greenhalgh v Arderne Cinemas Ltd* (1946). In this case the company had two classes of shares; 50 pence shares and 10 pence shares. The 50 pence shares carried one vote each as did the 10 pence shares. The resolution that was proposed was to sub-divide the 50 pence shares into 10 pence shares thus giving the shares in effect five times as many votes as previously. It was argued on behalf of the 10 pence shareholders that this constituted a variation of class rights and that their rights were being varied. The Court of Appeal took the view that this did not constitute a variation. The rights attaching to the 10 pence shares remained constant. They carried one vote per share. Such an approach is restrictive. Furthermore, it seems from the judgment of Lord Greene MR that had the approach been to limit the votes of the 10 pence shares to one vote for every five shares of that class that this would have been a variation. Lord Greene MR said:

Of course, if it had been attempted to reduce that voting right, eg by providing or attempting to provide that there should be one vote for every five of such shares, that would have been an interference with the voting rights attached to that class of shares. But nothing of the kind has been done; the right to have one vote per share is left undisturbed.

With all due respect to the learned judge something of the kind had been done. The practical effect of the variation is precisely the same in quintupling the votes of the 50 pence shareholders as in dividing the votes of the 10 pence shareholders by five. The approach is excessively legalistic.

Once it has been established that there has been a variation of class rights then the rules that have to be followed to carry the variation into effect are dependent upon where the rights are set out and what the rights concern. The rules are as follows:

- If the class rights are set out in the company's memorandum and the memorandum does not set out a variation procedure or if the variation procedure is set out in the articles of association, otherwise than on the company's initial incorporation, then modification of those rights can only be achieved by a scheme of arrangement under s 425 of the Companies Act 1985 or by all of the members of the company agreeing to the variation (s 125(4), (5) and (7) of the Companies Act 1985).

- If the class rights and the variation procedure are both set out in the memorandum then that procedure must be followed (s 17(2) of the Companies Act 1985).

- If the class rights are set out in the memorandum and that prohibits variation of the rights, then no variation can be effected except by a scheme of arrangement under s 425 of the Companies Act 1985 (s 17 of the Companies Act 1985).

- If the class rights are set out in the memorandum and the variation procedure is set out in the articles on initial incorporation then that procedure must be followed (s 125(4)(a) of the Companies Act 1985).

- If the class rights are set out otherwise than in the memorandum, for example, in the articles and the variation procedure is set out in the articles then that procedure must be followed (s 125(4)(b) of the Companies Act 1985).

- If the class rights are attached to a class of shares other than by the company's memorandum and the company's articles do not contain provision in respect of their alteration, they may be altered by the statutory variation procedure set out in s 125(2) of the

Companies Act 1985 whereby the holders of 75% of the nominal value of the issued shares of the class in question consent or an extraordinary resolution which sanctions the variation is passed at a separate general meeting of the shareholders of that class.

- There are special rules that apply if the class rights are set out in the memorandum or otherwise and the variation procedure is contained in the memorandum or articles if the rights are connected with the giving, variation, revocation or renewal of an authority for the purposes of s 80 of the Companies Act 1985 (allotment of securities by directors), or the reduction of share capital under s 135 of the Companies Act 1985. In this situation whatever procedure is set out, the statutory procedure of s 125(2) must be followed.

If the class rights are varied under a procedure set out in the memorandum or articles of the company or if the class rights are set out otherwise than in the memorandum and the articles are silent on variation, then dissentient minorities have special rights to object to the alteration. They must satisfy certain conditions. The dissenters must hold no less than 15% of the issued shares of the class and must not have voted in favour of the resolution. They may then object to the variation within 21 days of consent being given to the resolution. On occasion their objections may be upheld by the court (s 125 of the Companies Act 1985).

Nothing could better illustrate the great mess that British company law sometimes gets itself into. This morass of rules is unnecessarily complicated. It is confusing to the specialist lawyer let alone to the average businessman. This surely must be an area that is ripe for reform and simplification. For the examination candidate it is a headache to learn these detailed rules.

- In addition to the various statutory restrictions considered above the power to alter a company's articles is subject to the overriding principle that any alteration must be bona fide for the benefit of the company as a whole.

In *Allen v Gold Reefs of West Africa Ltd* (1900) the company's articles originally provided:

... that the company shall have a first and paramount lien for all debts obligations and liabilities of any member to or towards the company upon all shares (not being fully paid) held by such member ...

The alteration proposed was to delete the words 'not being fully paid' to provide the company with a lien over any shares of a member where a debt was due from that member. The alteration was challenged. Lindley MR said as follows:

Wide, however, as the language of s 50 is (now s 9 of the Companies Act 1985), the power conferred by it must, like all other powers, be exercised subject to those general principles of law and equity which are applicable to all powers conferred on majorities and enabling them to bind minorities' stock. It must be exercised, not only in the manner required by law, but also bona fide for the benefit of the company as a whole, and it must not be exceeded. These conditions are always implied, and are seldom, if ever, expressed. But if they are complied with I can discover no grounds for judicially putting any other restrictions on the power conferred by the section and those contained in it.

In the instant case the Court of Appeal held that the power had been exercised *bona fide*.

Much of the case law in this area centres upon a discussion as to how one determines whether the alteration is for the benefit of the company as a whole. In *Greenhalgh v Arderne Cinemas Ltd* (1951) (a later case involving the same parties as the case mentioned on p 31) it was proposed to delete a pre-emption provision in the company's articles. The majority shareholder, Mr Mallard, was prompted not by what was in the company's best interests but seemingly out of malice towards a minority shareholder. Lord Evershed MR in the Court of Appeal said:

Certain principles, I think, can be safely stated as emerging from those authorities. In the first place, I think it is now plain that 'bona fide for the benefit of the company as a whole' is not two things but one thing. It means that the shareholder must proceed upon what, in his honest opinion is for the benefit of the company as a whole. The second thing is that the phrase, 'the company as a whole', does not (at any rate in such a case as the present) mean the company as a commercial entity, distinct from the corporators: it means the corporators as a general body. That is to say, the case may be taken of an individual hypothetical member and it may be asked whether what is proposed, is, in the honest opinion of those who voted in its favour, for that person's benefit.

In this case the Court of Appeal held that the alteration was valid.

Difficulties remain in deciding what is for the benefit of the individual hypothetical member. Hardship to a minority would not automatically invalidate the alteration in question. In *Sidebottom v Kershaw Leese and Company Ltd* (1920) the Court of Appeal upheld an alteration which permitted the compulsory acquisition of the shares of a minority who was competing with the business of the company. It was held that an alteration permitting such an acquisition was valid even though it was carried out specifically against a particular member. This decision should be contrasted with *Brown v British Abrasive Wheel Company* (1919). In this case a 98% majority shareholder wished to insert a provision in the articles requiring the minority who were not prepared to invest further capital in the company to sell their shares as a condition of the majority's subscribing further capital. This alteration was held invalid. In this case the power could be used by the majority against the minority.

It is extremely rare for the courts to uphold an objection to an alteration of a company's articles on the grounds that it is not *bona fide* for the benefit of the company as a whole.

Sections 459 to 461 of the Companies Act 1985 do provide a possible remedy to a minority shareholder or indeed any shareholder who has been unfairly prejudiced in the conduct of a company's affairs by the use of voting powers. The courts have also sometimes been willing to act to protect minority shareholders from the oppressive use of majority voting power. This was the case in *Clemens v Clemens Brothers Ltd and Another* (1976) and *Estmanco (Kilner House) Ltd v Greater London Council* (1982) as well as in the unreported case *Pennell Securities Ltd v Venida Investments Ltd* (25 July 1974 noted by Burridge in (1981) 44 MLR 40).

A provision in the company's articles that an article (or articles) is unalterable is ineffective (see *Peters' American Delicacy Company Ltd v Heath* (1939)).

It should be re-emphasised that an alteration of the articles cannot be injuncted merely because it results in a breach of contract. The remedy will be in damages (see *Southern Foundries (1926) Ltd v Shirlaw* (1940)).

Issues involving alteration of the company's articles often feature on the examination paper. Look out for variation of class rights and remember, it is not always obvious that the company has more than one class of share.

The membership contract

A favourite examination topic is the membership contract between the members of the company and the company – the terms of a company's constitution which binds the company to its members and vice versa. This also constitutes a contract between the members *inter se*. This is set out in s 14 of the Companies Act 1985. This is no ordinary contract however and examination questions tend to focus upon the unique features of this contract.

The court has no jurisdiction to rectify the company's articles or memorandum of association even though they do not represent the intention of those signing them. This was the ratio in *Scott v Frank F Scott (London) Ltd* (1940). In that case it was contended by the defendants that the plaintiff was obliged to offer the shares of her deceased husband to them as the other shareholders of the company. It was argued on their behalf that the articles of association should be rectified so as to provide that all ordinary shares of a deceased member should be offered by his executors or administrators to the principal shareholders of the company. It was held that rectification has no part to play in relation to the membership contract. Luxmoore LJ said:

> It seems to us that there is no room in the case of a company incorporated under the appropriate statute or statutes for the application to either the memorandum or articles of association of the principles upon which a Court of Equity permits rectification of documents whether *inter partes* or not. The memorandum and articles of association of any company which it is proposed to incorporate must be signed by the requisite number of persons who desire its incorporation and must comply with the statutory requirements in respect of registration.

In this respect the contract is quite different from a normal contract. However, if the understanding of the members differs materially from the constitutional arrangements of the company, this may be a basis for winding the company up on the just and equitable ground under s 122(1)(g) of the Insolvency Act 1986. In the New Zealand case of *Re North End Motels (Huntly) Ltd* (1976) a retired farmer subscribed for half of the company on the basis that he would have a say in running the company. He found that he was in a minority on the board of directors and effectively had no say in running the company. He successfully petitioned to wind the company up on the just and equitable ground.

It was formerly the case that a member of a company could not sue for damages for breach of his membership contract while remaining a member of the company. This was a somewhat unusual feature of the membership contract of a company. A member was limited to the remedy of an injunction or a declaration. This was the rule in *Houldsworth v City of Glasgow Bank* (1880). However, s 131 of the Companies Act 1989, amending the Companies Act 1985 (s 111A), now provides:

> ... a person is not debarred from obtaining damages or other compensation from a company by reason only of his holding or having held shares in the company or any right to apply or subscribe for shares or to be included in the company's register in respect of shares.

The s 14 contract is, of course, alterable by special resolution in most situations (see above). This therefore means that the terms of the s 14 contract are alterable . The s 14 contract is, of course, also subject to the provisions of the Companies Act and other legislation.

Upon a literal reading of s 14 it appears simply to create contractual rights and obligations between the company and its members and between members *inter se*. However, the section has been interpreted in some cases as only creating rights and duties in respect of membership (or qua member). In the leading case of *Hickman v Kent or Romney Marsh Sheep Breeders Association* (1915) there was an obligation to submit membership disputes to arbitration under Article 49 of the company's articles of association. In this situation Astbury J said:

> ... in the present case the plaintiff's action is, in substance, to enforce his rights as a member under the articles against the association. Article 49 is a general article applying to all the members as such, and, apart from technicalities, it would seem reasonable that the plaintiff will not be allowed in the absence of any evidence filed by him to proceed with an action to enforce his rights under the articles, seeing that the action is a breach of his obligation under Article 49 to submit his dispute with the association to arbitration ...

The High Court decision has been accepted in later cases. It was accepted in *Beattie v E&F Beattie Ltd* (1938) by the Court of Appeal where a member who was sued in his capacity as a director rather than as a member was held not to be entitled to rely on the statutory contract to refer a dispute to arbitration. If this interpretation of the section in *Hickman and Beattie* is correct then the contract can only be invoked in respect of membership rights and obligations and not, for example, in disputes between officers and the company. Thus, in *Eley v Positive Government Security Life Assurance Company* (1876) the articles provided that Eley should be solicitor to the company. He was a member of the company but was unable to enforce the article in his capacity as company solicitor.

In *Pender v Lushington* (1877) a member was able to restrain a company from acting on the basis that he could not demand a poll of the members and in *Wood v Odessa Waterworks Company* (1889) a member was able to enforce the terms of the articles to have a dividend paid in cash.

Professor Gower espouses the view that s 14 can only be utilised qua member:

> ... the decisions have constantly affirmed that the section confers contractual effect on a provision in the memorandum and articles only in so far as it affords rights or imposes obligations on a member qua member.

> (*Gower's Principles of Modern Company Law*,
> 6th edn, Sweet & Maxwell, p 118).

A contrary view is put forward in an article in the *Cambridge Law Journal* by Lord Wedderburn in 'Shareholders Rights and the Rule in *Foss v Harbottle*' [1957] CLJ 194. In this article Lord Wedderburn argues that the decision in *Quinn & Axtens v Salmon* (1909) permitting a member to obtain an injunction restraining the company from concluding agreements entered into in breach of the company's articles showed that the member was able to enforce his rights as a director.

The cases are difficult to reconcile.

In the *Modern Law Review* ((1972) 35 MLR 362) GN Goldberg argues that a member has a contractual right to have the affairs of the company conducted by the particular organ of the company specified in the act or the company's constitution. Dr Dan Prentice by contrast argues that a member qua member can sue the company where the particular provision affects the power of the company to function ((1980) 1 Co Law 179). It is probably impossible to square the decided cases with any one view.

Roger Gregory probably comes close to the truth when he argues ((1981) 44 MLR 526) that the older case law is confused and inconsistent.

Drury ([1986] CLJ 219) takes a view that is similar to that of Lord Wedderburn.

It has been noted that the membership contract is also enforceable between members *inter se*. This was the ratio of the decision in *Rayfield v Hands* (1963). In *London Sack & Bag Ltd v Dixon & Lugton* (1943) the court refused to enforce a provision in the company's constitution between two members as it did not concern them as members. This returns us to the debate between Professor Gower and Lord Wedderburn.

On occasion the company's memorandum and articles may form the basis of a quite separate contract. This happened in *Re New British Iron Company ex p Beckwith* (1898) where directors of the company were able to imply a contract on the same terms as the articles when suing for their fees.

However, if this is the case then the contract incorporating the terms of the company's articles may well be determined to be on alterable terms since the articles are freely alterable. Thus, in *Swabey v Port Darwin Gold Mining Company* (1889) the court took the view that the company could alter its articles and so effect the terms of the contract for the future.

Where there is a contract on the same terms as the articles there may be an implied term that the contract is fixed at a particular date so that the contract is not freely alterable (see *Southern Foundries (1926) Ltd v Shirlaw* (1940)).

It may, therefore, be seen how the s 14 contract differs from an orthodox type of contract. The examiner often delights in such distinctions. This area lends itself to essay questions but it may also feature as part of a problem question.

3 Capital

> **You should be familiar with the following areas:**
>
> - promoters and their duties
> - pre-incorporation contracts
> - raising finance from the public – prospectuses and listing particulars
> - rules relating to payment for shares
> - rules relating to the maintenance of capital
> - the payment of dividends and constraints upon paying dividends

Introduction

Likely examination areas are reviewed in depth.

Promoters

Promoters, pre-incorporation contracts, prospectuses and listing particulars are a favourite examination topic. Very often they are linked together so that in a problem two or more of these areas may combine.

It is first proposed to look at the area of promoters. Professor Gower in *Principles of Modern Company Law* talks of the hey day of the professional company promoter in Edwardian Britain. He notes that in the popular imagination a company promoter would probably be a character of dubious repute and antecedents who infests the commercial demi-monde and who, after rising to affluence by preying on the susceptibilities of a gullible public, finally retires from the scene in the blaze of a sensational suicide or Old Bailey trial. Such is far from the truth today. The archetypal company promoter is an individual who is converting his own business into a private limited company. He is not a professional, he is merely incorporating his business.

There is no satisfactory definition of a promoter. There is no definition in any of the relevant statutes. It is wise, however, to be familiar with some of the dicta in the cases as questions often revolve around the question of whether a particular individual in a problem is a promoter or not. In *Twycross v Grant* (1877) Cockburn CJ defined a company promoter as a person who 'undertakes to form a company with reference to a given project and to set it going and who take the necessary steps to accomplish that purpose'. In *Emma Silver Mining Company v Grant* (1879) Lord Lindley said that the term had 'no very definite meaning'. The question of whether a person is a promoter or not is a question of fact.

Inevitably, if questions involve promoters there will be an issue relating to the duties of the promoters. Promoters owe fiduciary duties to the company which they are promoting. The duties are very similar to those owed by directors to their company and by trustees to their trust.

A promoter must not, therefore, make a profit out of the promotion unless it is disclosed to the company and unless the company agrees to his retention of the profits. The promoter should disclose any profits that he is making from the promotion either to an independent board of directors as discussed in *Erlanger v New Sombrero Phosphate Co* (1878) or, alternatively, disclosure may be made to all of the shareholders, actual and potential as in *Salomon v A Salomon* (1897).

The duty of disclosure is a duty to disclose all profits, whether direct or indirect. Thus, in *Gluckstein v Barnes* (1900) where the promoter failed to disclose a profit that he had made by buying up a mortgage at a discount he was held liable to disgorge that profit back to the company.

Another aspect of the fiduciary duties of promoters is that if a promoter acquires property during a promotion period, then he holds that property on trust for the company. There appears to be no British case which has this as the *ratio decidendi*. However, there are *dicta* in *Ladywell Mining Co v Brookes* (1887) to that effect.

Where full disclosure of any profits has not been made, then various remedies are open to the company in the normal run of events. First the company may seek to rescind the contract with the promoter. The remedy of rescission is, however, subject to the normal bars to that remedy. Thus, there can be no rescission if there has been affirmation of the contract, if third party rights have intervened or if restitution of the property is no longer possible. A second possible remedy is to recover the profit from the promoter rather than to rescind the contract. These two remedies are alternatives. Thus, in *Gluckstein v Barnes* (1900), recovery of the indirect profit was granted to the company. The remedy of disgorgement is not available where the promoter has acquired the property in a pre-promotion period. In such a situation, not all of the profit that has accrued is rightly the company's, even where there has been no disclosure. The profit that is attributable to the pre-promotion period should surely belong to the promoter (or the non-promoter as he then was!). The courts will not intervene in a situation such as this to try to apportion the profits. Instead, it seems that in such a situation the only remedy that is available is that of rescission (see *Re Cape Breton Co, Cavendish Bentinck v Fenn* (1887) and *Ladywell Mining Co v Brookes* (1887)).

On occasion, it may be that neither of these remedies is available. This would be the case, for example, if the property was acquired pre-promotion so that some of the profit is attributable to a pre-promotion period and if the remedy of rescission is blocked for one of the reasons set out above.

In one case the remedy of damages was made available to the company. The company was awarded the difference between the market price and the contract price where the company paid over the odds for the property. The property in question was the purchase of two music halls (*Re Leeds and Hanley Theatre of Varieties* (1902)).

Particular problems arise in relation to the remuneration of promoters. There can be no obligation in contract between the promoter and the company. The company is not in existence and therefore cannot have entered into any contract with the promoter (see *Re National Motor-Mail Coach Co Ltd (Clinton's Claim)* (1908)).

A promoter may be disqualified from acting as a director, liquidator, administrative receiver or administrator, or being otherwise involved in the business. Under the Company Directors' Disqualification Act 1986, an order may be made against any person. All disqualifications are subject to this Act. The disqualification may in extreme cases last for up to 15 years.

Pre-incorporation contracts

As has been mentioned, an area that is often coupled with promoters is that of pre-incorporation contracts. This is the situation where a person enters into a contract on behalf of an as yet unformed company.

The position used to be somewhat confused. Before the European Communities Act 1972, the position seemed to depend upon what particular formula was used by the person entering into the contract on behalf of the unformed company. If the person entered into the contract signing for and on behalf of the company, then personal liability would result. Thus in *Kelner v Baxter* (1866), the plaintiff had delivered goods to the defendant. The goods had been ordered on behalf of the proposed Gravesend Royal Alexandra Hotel Co Ltd. The question arose as to whether the company was liable. It was held that the company could not be liable since it did not exist at the time but the defendant acting on behalf of the unformed company was held liable on the contract.

By contrast, if the person entered into the contract signing his name and adding after his name the description of the office that he will hold when the company is incorporated, then no liability would arise as there was no contract. This was the position in *Newborne v Sensolid (Great Britain) Ltd* (1954). In this case, the company purported to sell a quantity of ham to the defendant. The defendant refused to take delivery of the ham. The company sued for breach of contract but as the company had not been registered until after the contract was concluded and as the plaintiff had signed his name together with the description as director, it was held that there could be no liability.

It also follows that where there can be no agency on behalf of an unformed company, since there is no principal in existence, there can be no ratification in this case either. This was the decision of the *Privy Council in Natal Land & Colonisation Co Ltd v Pauline Colliery & Development Syndicate Ltd* (1904). This was an appeal from the Supreme Court of Natal. The court took the view that ratification was not possible and in such a situation the company should enter into a completely new contract and the old contract should be discharged. It is worth noting in passing that many countries have provided by statute that a pre-incorporation contract can be ratified by a company when it comes into existence. The Companies Bill 1973 in Clause 6 would have made a similar provision but the bill failed.

Section 9(2) of the European Communities Act 1972, now s 36C(1) of the Companies Act 1985 provides:

- a contract which purports to be made by or on behalf of a company at a time when the company has not been formed, has effect, subject to any agreement to the contrary, as one made with the person purporting to act for the company or as agent for it, and he is personally liable on that contract accordingly.

In *Phonogram Ltd v Lane* (1982), the court had to consider the effect of this section where a company called Fragile Management Ltd was in the process of being incorporated. The company was to manage a pop group called Cheap, Mean and Nasty. The defendant was the manager of the pop group. He agreed with the plaintiffs that the plaintiffs would supply finance. He signed an agreement undertaking to repay the monies that had been advanced on behalf of Fragile Management Ltd if the contract were not completed before a certain date. Subsequently, the plaintiff sued the defendant for the money that had been advanced. The defendant argued that he was not personally liable on the agreement. It was suggested on his behalf that the contract was not 'purported' to be made by the company as it was known that the company was not in existence. Indeed it was known by both parties that the company had not yet been formed. However, Lord Denning MR took the view, a view shared by other members of the Court of Appeal, that a contract can purport to be made on behalf of a company, even though the company is known by both parties to the agreement not to have been formed. He took the view that the section could only be excluded by express contrary agreement. The other members of the Court of Appeal shared this view.

Prospectuses and listing particulars

It is most unusual for examiners to require students to know the detailed rules relating to the content of listing particulars and prospectuses. In relation to prospectuses (which are those documents prepared by companies offering shares or debentures to the public which are not listed on the official list of the Stock Exchange), the rules are set out in the Public Offers of Securities Regulations 1995.

In relation to listing particulars (the document produced by companies that are quoted on the official list of the Stock Exchange which are offering shares or debentures to the public), the detailed rules are set out in the Stock Exchange Yellow Book (the rules on admission of securities to listing). Section 146 of the Financial Services Act 1986 provides in relation to listing particulars that 'in addition to the information specified by listing rules or required by the competent authority as a condition of the admission of any securities to the official list, any listing particulars submitted to the competent authority ... shall contain all such information as investors and their professional advisers would reasonably require, and reasonably expect to find there, for the purpose of making an informed assessment of:

- the assets and liabilities, financial position, profits and losses, and prospects of the issue of the securities; and
- the rights attaching to those securities.'

Most questions involving a consideration of prospectuses or listing particulars require an assessment of the remedies that may be available to a misled investor.

The statutory remedy for those who suffer loss as a result of misleading listing particulars is set out in s 150 of the Financial Services Act. Any investor who purchases securities and suffers loss as a result of misleading listing particulars is eligible for compensation, unless one of the defences applies.

Where a misleading prospectus is issued Regulations 13 and 15 of the Public Offers of Securities Regulations 1995 provide a similar remedy

There are, of course, other remedies available to those subscribing for or purchasing shares as a result of misleading listing particulars or prospectuses. It makes no difference, however, whether the purchaser or subscriber has relied upon either a prospectus or listing particulars in this regard.

Thus, the remedy of rescission may be available where a person subscribes for shares on the basis of misleading listing particulars or a misleading prospectus. The usual bars to rescission will apply. Thus, if there has been affirmation, or the intervention of third party rights, or if restitution is not possible, rescission will not be available. Obviously, the remedy of rescission is only available to a subscriber against the company, the other contracting party.

If the plaintiff has been induced to purchase shares or debentures on the basis of a misleading prospectus or misleading listing particulars, he may have a remedy for the misrepresentation under statute. It has already been seen that he may seek rescission. In addition, damages may be available in lieu of rescission, see s 2(2) of the Misrepresentation Act 1967. Obviously, these damages can only be awarded if rescission is available.

Section 2(1) of the Misrepresentation Act 1967 provides that damages may be awarded where loss has occurred through a misrepresentation, unless the misrepresentor can prove that he had reasonable grounds to believe, and did believe, up to the time the contract was made that the facts represented were true. The section only applies if the misrepresentor is a party to the contract. It therefore means that the remedy is only available to a subscriber for shares.

A remedy may be available in tort. In relation to tortious remedies, it is conceivable that the remedy may be available both to a subscriber purchasing shares or debentures directly from the company and a purchaser on the open market who buys from another person after relying upon the content of the prospectus or listing particulars. The plaintiff may seek to obtain damages in the tort of deceit. He would need to show that there is a statement of fact which is fraudulent or which is made recklessly as to its truth. In *Derry v Peek* (1889), a prospectus was issued by a tramway company. The company was empowered to use horse-drawn trams in Plymouth. The prospectus stated that the company was empowered to use steam-driven vehicles. This was not the case. Permission was not granted in relation to a request that had been made. It was held that since the directors honestly believed the statement to be true, they were not liable for fraud. An action in the tort of deceit may be brought against the company itself or against the directors. Since the remedy in contract is available against the company itself, it is not likely to be used by a subscriber for shares. It may, however, be used where a purchaser of shares on the open market wishes to bring an action in tort where he cannot bring one in contract. He would need to demonstrate that the prospectus or listing particulars are designed to encourage purchases of shares on the open market, see *Andrews v Mockford* (1896). In this case the Court of Appeal considered that the prospectus was designed to induce application for both the allotment of shares from the public and for the purchase of shares in the open market.

An action will also lie in damages for the tort of negligent misstatement. In such an instance, it must be shown that the company owes a duty of care to the investor. It will, however, be easier to demonstrate negligence as opposed to deceit. Once again, it will be necessary to demonstrate if the investor is a purchaser in the open market that the prospectus or listing particulars was designed to encourage the purchase of shares on the open market.

These are the most important matters to consider in relation to prospectuses and listing particulars so far as the examination is concerned. It will also be useful to be familiar with the provisions in relation to criminal liability.

First, it should be noted that s 202(1) of the Financial Services Act 1986 provides that where an offence is committed by a company and is proved to have been committed with the consent or connivance of, or to be attributable to, any neglect on the part of any director, manager, secretary or other similar officer of the company, or any person who is purporting to act in any such capacity, or a controller of the company, he as well as the body corporate shall be guilty of that offence and liable to be proceeded against and punished accordingly.

If a person involved in carrying on an investment business issues false listing particulars or a false prospectus, he will be guilty of an offence in certain situations under s 47 of the Financial Services Act 1986. If such a person makes a statement, promise or forecast which he knows to be misleading, false or deceptive, or dishonestly conceals any material facts or recklessly makes (dishonestly or otherwise) a statement, promise or forecast which is misleading, false or deceptive, if it is for the purpose of inducing another to enter into any investment agreement, he is guilty of an offence. The section also makes it an offence to do any act or engage in conduct creating a false or misleading impression as to the market in or value of any investment if it is done to induce another to acquire, dispose of, subscribe for or underwrite those investments or to refrain from doing so or to exercise or refrain from exercising any rights conferred by those investments. It is a defence if the person concerned can prove that he reasonably believed that his act or conduct would not create an impression that was false or misleading. The maximum penalty is seven years' imprisonment.

Under s 154 of the Financial Services Act 1986, it is an offence to publish an advertisement of securities without the approval of the Stock Exchange. An authorised person under the Act who contravenes the section is liable to disciplinary action whereas an unauthorised person is liable to up to two years' imprisonment and/or a fine on indictment. This applies also to prospectuses (s 154A of the Act).

A copy of listing particulars must be deposited with the registrar of companies. Failure to do so is an offence under s 149(3) of the Financial Services Act 1986, punishable on indictment by a fine. This too applies to prospectuses (s 154A of the Act).

It is an offence for a private company to issue an advertisement offering its securities to the public (s 81 of the Companies Act 1985).

Section 19 of the Theft Act 1968 provides that an officer or person purporting to act as such with the intention of deceiving members or creditors of a company publishes a statement or account which he knows is, or may be, misleading is guilty of an offence. This carries a maximum sentence of seven years' imprisonment.

Rules relating to payment for shares

The following matters should be checked where shares are to be issued by a public or a private company:

- does the company have sufficient authorised share capital for the issue? This may be checked by looking at the company's memorandum. If necessary, the authorised capital may be increased, see s 121 of the Companies Act 1985;
- do the directors have authority to allot the shares? See s 80 of the Companies Act 1985. Note, a private company may pass an elective resolution that s 80 is not to apply to that company since normally authority under s 80 can only last up to five years (see Chapter 5);
- do pre-emption rights apply? Section 89 of the Companies Act 1985 makes statutory provision for pre-emption on second and subsequent issues of shares. This may be excluded by a private company in its constitution, see s 91 of the Companies Act 1985. It may be excluded by both public and private companies by special resolution, see s 95(2) of the Companies Act 1985;
- the rules for payment for shares are based upon the second EC directive on company law. These rules are incorporated into the Companies Act 1985.

Section 99(1) of the Companies Act 1985 requires that shares should be paid up in money or in money's worth.

Section 99(2) of the Companies Act 1985 provides that a public company cannot accept an undertaking from a person to do work or perform services for shares.

Section 100 of the Companies Act 1985 requires that shares cannot be issued at a discount. This applies to both public and private companies. There are, however, four exceptions to this principle:

(a) shares may be issued to underwriters at a discount of up to 10%, see s 97 of the Companies Act 1985;

(b) convertible debentures may be issued at a discount provided there is no immediate right to conversion (see *Koffyfontein Mines Limited v Mosely* (1911));

(c) shares may be issued in exchange for services that happen to be overvalued in a private company. Shares may not be issued in exchange for services in a public company;

(d) shares may be issued in exchange for property which is overvalued in a private company. In a public company, there is a need for an independent expert valuation of the property concerned (see s 103 of the Companies Act 1985).

In a public company, shares must be paid up to at least one-quarter of their nominal value, plus the whole of any premium (s 101 of the Companies Act 1985).

A public company cannot issue shares in exchange for a non-cash consideration which may be transferred more than five years from the date of allotment (s 102(1) of the Companies Act 1985).

Where shares are issued at a premium (ie above their nominal value) in either a private or public company, the whole of the premium is placed in a share premium account. This is treated as if it were ordinary share capital for most purposes. It cannot be used to pay off a dividend. However, it may be used to pay up a bonus issue of shares (s 130 of the Companies Act 1985).

Rules relating to the maintenance of capital

Companies are prohibited from purchasing their own shares, subject to certain exceptions (see s 143 of the Companies Act 1985).

Section 159 of the Companies Act 1985 allows companies to issue redeemable shares of any class subject to restrictions.

Section 162 of the Companies Act 1985 allows companies to purchase their own shares subject to certain restrictions.

Public companies can only redeem or purchase their own shares out of profits or out of the proceeds of a fresh issue of shares. Private companies may purchase out of capital, subject to certain safeguards (see s 171 of the Companies Act 1985).

Companies are generally prohibited from providing financial assistance towards the purchase of their own shares, see s 151 of the Companies Act 1985. There are exceptions to this principle. In particular, private companies may provide financial assistance out of distributable profits (see s 155 of the Companies Act 1985, and *Brady v Brady* (1989)).

Companies may reduce their capital by passing a special resolution to this effect and obtaining the consent of the court to the reduction (see s 135 of the Companies Act 1985).

The payment of dividends

Until the Companies Act 1980, there was no statutory intervention in this area. The rules were somewhat confused, in particular the definition of a profit was uncertain.

Following the second EC directive on company law, statutory rules were introduced in the Companies Act 1980, now consolidated into the Companies Act 1985.

Section 263 of the Companies Act 1985 provides that distributions can only be made out of accumulated realised profits less accumulated realised losses.

Note – the profits and losses must be 'accumulated', overruling the position in *Ammonia Soda Company v Chamberlain* (1918).

The profit must be 'realised', overruling the decision in *Dimbula Valley (Ceylon) Tea Company Ltd v Laurie* (1961).

Section 264 of the Companies Act 1985 applies to public companies only. It requires the public company to maintain the capital side of its account in addition to having available profits. Therefore, if the company's net assets are worth less than the subscribed shared capital, plus undistributable reserves at the end of the trading period, that shortfall must first be made good out of distributable profits before a dividend can be paid.

If a dividend is wrongly paid, a member may be liable to repay it under s 277 of the Companies Act 1985.

Directors who are responsible for unlawful distributions, could be liable for breach of duty (see *Flitcroft's Case* (1882)). If the directors have relied upon the auditors in recommending a dividend, then the auditors may well be liable (see *Dovey v Cory* (1901)).

4 The management of the company

You should be familiar with the following areas:

- procedures for the appointment and removal of directors
- the duties of directors
- legislation combating insider dealing
- the role and duties of the company secretary
- the role and duties of the company's auditors

Introduction

Certain areas are examination favourites. These are examined in depth.

Removal of directors

The key issue which is often examinable – sometimes in essay form and sometimes as part of a problem question – concerns the removal of directors.

What is now s 303 of the Companies Act 1985 provides that a director may always be removed from the board of directors by ordinary resolution in general meeting notwithstanding anything contained in his employment contract or anything contained in the company's constitution. This provision was first introduced in the Companies Act 1948 following recommendations of the Cohen Committee of 1945.

This may seem to be a very powerful weapon in the hands of shareholders but for various reasons discussed below it is not as powerful as it first seems.

The operation of the section was discussed in *Bushell v Faith* (1970). In this case, a small private company concerned with the management of a block of flats in Southgate, North London, was at the centre of the dispute. The shares were held by two sisters and a brother. The two sisters wished to remove the brother from the board of directors. Since the shares were held equally, on the face of it, this should present no problem. However, a provision in the company's articles of association stated that on a resolution to remove a director from office, his shares would carry three votes each. If this were valid, this would have the effect of entrenching the brother and preventing his removal. Nor would it be possible to alter the company's articles as this would require a special resolution. The House of Lords held by a majority of four to one that the provision was valid. The brother was therefore protected from removal.

In the same way, a provision in the company's constitution requiring a particular quorum at a meeting to remove a director would no doubt also be valid (see *Re BML Group Ltd* (1994)).

Section 303 is stated to be without prejudice to a director's rights to compensation for breach of any service agreement (see s 303(5) of the Companies Act 1985). Section 319 of the Companies Act 1985 does, however, provide that a director cannot have a service agreement for a period of more than five years unless the term is first approved by a resolution of the company in general meeting. This provision, therefore, to some extent counteracts the possibility of a director having a long service agreement at high remuneration and then suing for compensation if removed from the board of directors. It may, nevertheless, prove expensive for a private company, and indeed sometimes a public company, to remove a director from the board (see *Shindler v Northern Raincoat Co Ltd* (1961) and *Southern Foundries Ltd v Shirlaw* (1940)).

On occasion a company may place in its constitution a liquidated damages provision which states that if a director is removed from the board he is entitled to a set amount of compensation. Provided that this sum is not a penalty, the director may simply enforce this provision (see *Taupo Totara Timber Co Ltd v Rowe* (1978)). This was a Privy Council decision on appeal from New Zealand.

A director may enter into voting agreements with shareholders who may agree to vote as directed by him or to protect his position from removal. Such agreements, provided they are supported by consideration, would be enforceable by mandatory injunction (see *Stewart v Schwab* (1956) South Africa).

It was formally the case that in a quasi-partnership company such as the company in *Ebrahimi v Westbourne Galleries Ltd* (1973) where a director was removed from the board, he could petition to wind the company up on the just and equitable ground on the basis that it was contrary to the understanding reached when the company was formed. In *Ebrahimi*, he and Nazar had run a successful partnership business selling carpets and tapestries. The company had been incorporated and had thrived. Later, Nazar's son was introduced to the business and both he and Ebrahimi transferred shares to Nazar's son, George. Discord followed and Nazar and George removed Ebrahimi from the board of directors. They had a majority of the shares and votes. The profits of the business were paid out as director's salary rather than dividends. Exclusion from the board therefore hit Ebrahimi in the pocket as well as hurting his pride. He sought and obtained a winding up order under the Act. The House of Lords held unanimously that his petition should be granted.

Such situations are now unlikely. Section 125(2) of the Insolvency Act 1986 requires the court, if it is of the opinion that the petitioner is entitled to relief, to decide whether it is just and equitable that the company should be wound up, bearing in mind the possibility of other forms of relief. The court, if it comes to the conclusion that it would be just and equitable that the company should be wound up in the absence of any other remedy, must make a winding up order unless it is of the opinion that the petitioner is acting unreasonably in not pursuing that other remedy. In most situations it will surely be unreasonable to pursue the winding up remedy where there is a possibility of a successful petition under ss 459–61 of the Companies Act 1985. However, in *Virdi v Abbey Leisure Ltd* (1990), the court did consider that a refusal by the shareholder to accept an offer to buy his shares where he feared that the valuation would be wrong was not unreasonable.

There have been many successful petitions under ss 459–61 of the Companies Act 1985 on the grounds of removal from management. Most of the cases concern quasi-partnership companies. One successful petition was in *Re Bovey Hotel Ventures Ltd* (1981) (unreported). It seems that it is not inconceivable that a successful petition could be presented even for a public company (see *Re Blue Arrow plc* (1987)), although it is unlikely in the case of a public company that a petition on the basis of exclusion from management would be successful.

Wherever a director is to be removed under s 303, special notice must be served. Special notice is defined in s 379 of the Companies Act 1985. This is 28 days' notice of the resolution from the person who is proposing the removal. The notice is given by depositing a copy of the resolution at the company's registered office.

The resolution should then be forwarded forthwith to the director concerned. The director may make representations in writing which should then be circulated to every member of the company to whom notice of the meeting is to be sent. If it is not sent for some reason, the representations must be read out at the meeting. An exception to the requirement of circulation or oral presentation is if the representations contain defamatory matter in which case application should be made to the court which will then decide if it is thought appropriate to circulate or for the director to read out the representations.

The director also has a right to speak at the meeting where his removal is proposed in his own defence in addition to the circulation of the representations.

Mere serving of the special notice does not, of course, entitle the person serving the special notice to have the meeting called. If it were otherwise, a single shareholder with one share serving special notice could require the company to call what may be a very expensive meeting (see *Pedley v The Inland Waterways Association Ltd* (1977)). In this case, Pedley who was a solicitor proposed the removal of the entire board of the company. He served special notice on the company but the board refused to call the meeting. Pedley argued that this was a contravention of the provisions of the Act. The court held that it was not. In order to have a meeting called, a person must fit within one of the provisions for the calling of meetings.

Although the Companies Act 1989 has introduced a new written resolution procedure where members of a private company agree unanimously on a course of action, this does not apply to the removal of directors. The reason for this is that the director concerned has a right to speak in his own defence, a right which can only be guaranteed by the meeting itself.

There is much material here for answering a question on the removal of directors. Since there are many protections for directors, it lends itself to examination questions and students should therefore ensure that they know this area in detail.

Directors' duties

It is inconceivable that an examination paper in company law could be set without touching on the area of directors' duties. A question may take the form of an essay or may be in problem form, possibly involving other areas such as minority protection.

Directors' duties may be conveniently split into two parts: the directors' duty of care and skill and directors' fiduciary duties. The rules are largely common law and equitable rather than statutorily based. However, there are some rules in the Companies Act and elsewhere that are relevant to this area.

The first question that should be considered is to whom do directors owe their duties. It used to be a simple matter. Directors owed their duties to the company which was interpreted as meaning the providers of capital, ie the company's shareholders. This meant the shareholders as a body rather than individual shareholders. Thus, in *Percival v Wright* (1902), certain shareholders approached directors and asked if the directors would purchase their shares. Negotiations took place but the directors failed to mention that a take-over bid had been made for the company. This materially affected the value of the shares. The court held that there had been no breach of duty by the directors. The directors owed their duties to the body of shareholders rather than individual shareholders and premature disclosure of the take-over negotiations could well have amounted to a breach of duty. The decision would have been different if the approach had been made by the directors to the shareholders (see *Breiss v Woolley* (1954) and *Allen v Hyatt* (1914)).

The traditional perspective that directors owed their duties to the providers of capital has now been modified by statute. Section 309 of the Companies Act 1985 provides that:

- The matters to which the directors of a company are to have regard in the performance of their functions include the interests of the company's employees in general as well as the interests of its members.

- Accordingly, the duty imposed by this section on the directors of a company is owed by them to the company (and the company alone) and is enforceable in the same way as any other fiduciary duty owed to a company by its directors.

The Bullock Committee, the Committee of Enquiry on Industrial Democracy had recommended (Cmnd 6706) that directors' duties should be extended to take account of the interests of employees.

The provision might seem to be radical in that it extends the category of persons that directors should take account of to include the providers of labour, but in fact the duty is enforceable in the same way as other duties and therefore ultimately is only enforceable by the company, ie the board of directors or, on occasion, the shareholders.

It is perhaps worth noting in passing that s 719 of the Companies Act 1985 permits a company to make payments to its employees on ceasing to trade or on transferring the business. This was something that was previously *ultra vires* where there was no business that was capable of being benefited (see *Parke v Daily News Ltd* (1962)).

Sometimes *dicta* in the cases indicate other duties that may be owed by directors. On occasion, judges may make reference to a duty being owed to creditors. This was the case in *Liquidator of West Mercia Safetywear Ltd v Dodd* (1988), for example. There is, however, in general, no recognition at common law or in equity of duties being owed to creditors. Creditors are protected by provisions of the Insolvency Act 1986 and elsewhere.

The duty of care and skill

In the Forsyte Saga (The White Monkey), Soames Forsyte ponders on the duties of directors. 'What besides the drawing of fees and the drinking of tea are the duties of a director?' That was the point. And how far, if he failed in them, was he liable?'

Traditionally, the duty of care and skill has been interpreted in a way that places a very modest burden upon the shoulders of directors. The leading case is *Re City Equitable Fire & Insurance Co Ltd* (1925). In this case, the company had experienced serious shortfalls of funds. The managing director, Mr Bevan, was convicted of fraud. The liquidator sought to make other directors liable in negligence for failing to detect the frauds. Romer J in what has become the classic exposition on the duty of care and skill set out three propositions. They are as follows:

A director need not exhibit in the performance of his duties a greater degree of skill than may be reasonably expected from a person of his knowledge and experience. A director of a life insurance company, for instance, does not guarantee that he has the skill of an actuary or a physician. In the words of Lord Lindley MR, 'If the directors act within their powers, if they act with such care as is reasonably to be expected from them, having regard to their knowledge and experience, and if they act honestly for the benefit of the company they represent, they discharge both their equitable as well as their legal duty to the company' (*Lagunas Nitrate Co v Lagunas Syndicate* (1899)).

It is perhaps only another way of stating the same proposition to say that the directors are not liable for mere errors of judgment.

These are the words of Romer J. In relation to this principle the decision in *Re Denham & Co* (1883) is illustrative. In this case, a director had recommended the payment of a dividend out of capital. The director was held not liable in negligence. It was stated that he was a country gentleman not an accountant!

Section 13 of the Supply of Goods and Services Act 1982 introduced an implied term that the supplier of services would provide services of a reasonable standard. Directors were exempted from this provision before it even came into force. This is surely an indication of the fact that the nature of this first proposition had not changed in 1982.

In *Dorchester Finance Co Ltd v Stebbing* (1989), Foster J held three directors liable for negligence. Two of the directors were non-executive and one was an executive director. The judge found that the duty that applied to the executive and non-executive directors was the same.

There are some indications that the nature of the duty of care and skill is changing. Section 214 of the Insolvency Act 1986 provides for an objective standard of care in relation to directors and shadow directors where the company is insolvent and they ought to have recognised that fact. In some cases, it seems that s 214 has been used to try to establish an objective standard of care for directors across the board. Thus, in *Norman v Theodore Goddard* (1991), Hoffmann J accepted that the standard in s 214 applied generally in relation to directors. The same judge in *Re D'Jan of London Ltd* (1993) accepted that the duty of care applicable was that set out in s 214 of the Insolvency Act 1986.

The second proposition put forward by Romer J in *Re City Equitable* relates to the attention that has to be paid to the affairs of the company. He said:

A director is not bound to give continuous attention to the affairs of a company. His duties are of an intermittent nature to be performed at periodic board meetings and at meetings of any committee of the board upon which he happens to be placed. He is not, however, bound to attend all such meetings, though he ought to attend whenever, in the circumstances, he is reasonably able to do so.

An old illustration of this second proposition of Romer J is to be found in *Re Cardiff Savings Bank, Marquis of Bute's Case* (1892). The Marquis of Bute was appointed president and director of the Cardiff Savings Bank when he was only six months old. During the next 38 years he attended only one board meeting. During this time frauds were perpetrated by another director. The court held that the Marquis was not liable for breach of duty in failing to attend board meetings as he had never undertaken to do so.

The third proposition set out by Romer J is as follows:

In respect of all duties that, having regard for the exigencies of business, and the articles of association, may properly be left to some other official, a director is, in the absence of grounds for suspicion, justified in trusting that official to perform such duties honestly ...

This third proposition does not present problems. It does not seem out of place at the close of the 20th century in the way that the other two propositions which were first set out at the start of the 20th century do seem out of date.

In *Dovey & Metropolitan Bank (of England and Wales) Ltd v Cory* (1901) where a director had delegated the task of drawing up the accounts to others, it was held that he was entitled to rely on those accounts in recommending the payment of a dividend which was in fact made out of capital.

Fiduciary duties

Other types of duties owed by directors are often described within the umbrella term 'fiduciary duties'. Some of this area is covered by statute. In addition, there is a considerable body of case law on this area.

Whilst little may be expected historically from company directors in relation to care and skill, much is expected in terms of honesty and integrity.

Certain provisions of the Companies Act require a director to make disclosures. Section 317 of the Companies Act 1985 requires the director to disclose any interest that he has in a contract between himself and the company. The provision extends to connected persons. Connected persons are: the director's spouse or infant children, a company with whom the director is associated (that is to say, he controls more than 20% of the voting capital), a trustee of a trust whose beneficiaries include the director himself or a connected person, a partner of the director or of a connected person (see s 346 of the Companies Act 1985).

A shadow director is also required to comply with s 317 in the same way as a director.

Disclosure under s 317 should be to the full board. The section is not complied with by disclosing the matter to a sub-committee of the board. This principle is seen at play in the House of Lords' decision in *Guinness plc v Saunders & another* (1990).

Mere compliance with the section does not entitle a director to keep any profits. In order to keep the profit, the director must be able to rely on a provision in the company's constitution or have his retention of the profit ratified by the company in general meeting.

Some contracts require prior authorisation by the company in general meeting. Section 320 of the Companies Act 1985 applies to what are termed substantial property transactions. If the director or shadow director is to sell or purchase from the company one or more non-cash assets that are substantial, then prior approval in general meeting is needed. A transaction is substantial if the market value of the asset exceeds the lower of £100,000 or 10% of the company's net asset value (as set out in the last balance sheet). Transactions worth less than £2,000 are never substantial. Section 320 applies just as s 317 does to connected persons.

If the substantial property transaction does not receive prior authorisation or ratification within a reasonable period of its conclusion, then it is voidable at the instance of the company. The director concerned is liable to make good any profit to the company and to indemnify the company against any loss.

Section 323 prohibits a director of a company or a shadow director from buying options (whether put, call or put and call) on shares or debentures of the company or its holding company or any subsidiaries of the company or any subsidiary of its holding company if the shares or debentures are listed. The penalty for infringement is up to two years' imprisonment and/or a fine.

Section 324 of the Companies Act 1985 requires a director or shadow director to notify the company of any interest in the shares or debentures of the company or any subsidiary of the company or its holding company or a subsidiary of the company's holding company.

Some of the rules are contained in decided cases. A director must not place himself in a position where his duty to the company conflicts with his personal interest. If he does, he is obliged to favour the interest of the company rather than his own. The leading case in this area is *Regal (Hastings) v Gulliver* (1942). Regal owned a cinema in Hastings. The company's solicitor, Garston, considered it would be a sound business proposition to acquire two other cinemas in the town. He suggested this to the board of directors. The company itself could not afford the purchase. However, a scheme was devised where the company's solicitor, the directors and the company itself would each put up some of the funds for the purchase. The move was a successful one and the company prospered. Ultimately, the company was sold as a going concern to a purchaser. He purchased the company's shares. The company under its new management then commenced an action against the erstwhile directors for damages in respect of the profit that they had made on the sale of their shares. It was established that the directors had acted from prudent financial motives and there was no *mala fides*. The House of Lords held, however, that the directors had acquired the shares in exploitation of their position as directors. They had not obtained the consent of the company and were bound to disgorge the profit back to the company. It was unfortunate that they had sold the company as a going concern and thus put the purchaser in the position to bring the action. Had they simply sold the company's assets, the purchaser would have had no *locus standi* to bring the action.

The same principle is borne out in later decisions. In *Industrial Developments Consultants v Cooley* (1962), Cooley had been an architect with the East Midlands Gas Board. He left there to become a director of IDC. Whilst there, he was approached by the Eastern Gas Board. They wished him to design a gas holder for them at Ponders End. They did not wish to deal with IDC. They made it quite clear that the offer was only an offer to Cooley personally. Cooley went to his management and told them that he was desperately ill and sought leave to terminate his contract. This was agreed to and he then convalesced by designing the gas holder! Clearly Cooley was dishonest in this case and should perhaps not profit from his dishonesty. The judge, however, said that the profit that he had made on the contract should be disgorged back to IDC. He held that it was a corporate opportunity. This is unlikely as it was clear that the Eastern Gas Board would not deal with IDC.

A further decision in the same area is *Horcal Ltd v Gatland* (1984). Gatland, a director of the company, was close to retirement. The board of directors had decided to award him a golden handshake. After the decision had been reached, Gatland took a phone call from a potential customer of the company. He converted the business to his own account. This came to light later when the customer rang the company to complain about the quality of the work. The company brought this action, partly to obtain disgorgement of the profit made and partly to obtain a return of the golden handshake payment. The company succeeded in obtaining disgorgement of the profit. It would have been surprising had they not so succeeded. They did not obtain a return of the golden handshake payment, however. It was held that this payment had been decided prior to the director diverting the contract. At the time of the diversion there were evil thoughts but no evil deeds! The decision is a surprising one. Had the directors known of the intention of Gatland to divert the contract, it seems unlikely that they would have pressed ahead with the golden handshake payment.

Often the decisions are more straightforward. In *Cranleigh Precision Engineering v Bryant* (1964), the director concerned had been working on a revolutionary above ground swimming pool. He left the company, taking plans with him, and developed a swimming pool of his own based on the plans. The company brought the action to seek disgorgement of profits that he had made and was successful.

Not every case of a director taking an opportunity that has come by way of the company will involve a breach of duty. If the company has turned down the opportunity without any improper influence from the director and the director takes it up subsequently, there is no reason why the director should not retain the profit. In *Peso Silver Mines v Cropper* (1966), before the Supreme Court of Canada, the court held that a director was entitled to keep a profit in these circumstances. In *Island Export Finance Ltd v Umunna* (1986), the judge said the question of whether a director was liable to disgorge a profit to his former company from a corporate opportunity was to some extent a question of timing. The director in this case had resigned from the company and set up in business on his own account. At the time, there were no specific corporate opportunities. It was held that in these circumstances Umunna could take the business that came his way even from previous customers.

The area of corporate opportunities is a fertile one for examiners, particularly in relation to problem questions. This area, therefore, deserves special attention.

A related area is the question of competition. To what extent is a director of the company able to compete with the company of which he is a director, either through another company or possibly through a partnership, or indeed trading as a sole trader? The old British case of *London & Mashonaland Exploration Co Ltd v New Mashonaland Exploration Co Ltd* (1891) puts forward the proposition that it does not involve a breach of duty. The decision is surprising although it was approved *obiter* by Lord Blanesburgh in *Bell v Lever Bros* (1932).

Logic would suggest that the proposition is untenable. If a corporate opportunity comes the way of a director, if he is a director of two companies he will inevitably be in breach of duty to one company where he diverts it to the other. He would be in breach to both companies if he chose not to divert it to either company.

Commonwealth authority is inconsistent on the point. Some cases follow the *Mashonaland* decision. Others indicate that directors cannot compete with their companies (see *Abbey Glen Property Corporation v Stumborg* (1976) (Canada)).

In some areas of British law, there is an indication that competition is not permissible. In *Hivac Ltd v Park Royal Scientific Instruments Ltd* (1946), senior employees engaged on sensitive work in wartime were not able to compete with their employer. Admittedly this is a special decision.

In partnership law, which sometimes provides an analogy with company law, competition is not permitted.

The *Mashonaland* decision is reviewed and criticised cogently by Michael Christie in the 1992 volume of the *Modern Law Review*.

Inevitably directors have powers in relation to the running of the company. Some of these will be implied by virtue of the office they hold. Others will be set out in the company's constitution. In relation to companies with share capital, one of the most important powers is the power to issue shares.

This power is given for the purpose of raising necessary capital for the running of the company. If this is the purpose for which it is used, it is clearly a valid exercise of the power. Other purposes, such as, for example, staving off an unwelcome take-over bid depends upon the company in general meeting. This was the case in *Hogg v Cramphorn Ltd* (1967) and *Bamford v JC Bamford* (1970).

If the exercise of the power is for some extraneous purpose to benefit the directors and not to benefit the company, then the issue of the shares cannot be validated by the company in general meeting (see *Howard Smith Ltd v Ampol Petroleum Ltd* (1974) (a Privy Council appeal from Australia).

If an issue of shares is made to disturb an existing balance of control within a company, then it may be held invalid. This happened in *Pennell Securities Ltd v Venida Investments Ltd* (1974), noted in [1981] MLR 40 by Susan Burridge. Similarly in *Clemens v Clemens Brothers Ltd* (1976) an issue of shares made to dilute the voting power of one shareholder was held invalid.

Thus directors' powers must be exercised in a fiduciary way. This is illustrated by these cases concerning the issue of shares but may be demonstrated in other areas. In *Re Smith & Fawcett Ltd* (1942), the same principle applied in relation to the directors' power to refuse to register a transfer of shares. More recently it applied in relation to entry into a management agreement in *Lee Panavision Ltd v Lee Lighting Ltd* (1992).

Nor should it be forgotten that even if there is no breach of directors' duties, there may still be a shareholder's petition under ss 459–61 of the Companies Act 1985.

The whole area of directors' duties is a vital one in examination preparation. It is one area which a student cannot afford to omit in his preparation for examinations. Some areas are self-contained and may lend themselves to strategic omission. This cannot be said of the area of directors' duties.

Directors' personal liability

Contract

Directors may be liable in contract for:
• breach of warranty of authority;
• a collateral guarantee;
• pre-incorporation contracts under s 36C(1) of the Companies Act 1985.

Tort

Directors may be liable in tort:
• for fraud in relation to listing particulars and prospectuses (see *Derry v Peek* (1889));
• for negligent misstatement in relation to listing particulars and prospectuses (see *Hedley Byrne v Heller* (1964));
• for a breach of a personal duty of skill and care (see *Fairline Shipping Corporation v Adamson* (1975) and *Williams v Natural Life Health Foods Limited* (1997)).

Statute

Directors may be liable under statute:
• for misstatements or omissions in listing particulars, see s 150 of the Financial Services Act 1986. Note also the position under the Public Offers of Securities Regulations 1995;
• for improper use of the company name, see s 349(4) of the Companies Act 1985.

Directors may be liable also under certain other legislative provisions including:
• s 213 of the Insolvency Act 1986 in relation to fraudulent trading;

- s 214 of the Insolvency Act 1986 in relation to wrongful trading;
- s 216 of the Insolvency Act 1986 in relation to phoenix companies using prohibited names (see *Thorne v Silverleaf* (1994));
- under other legislation, particularly affecting health and safety and the environment such as the Health and Safety at Work Act 1974, the Control of Pollution Act 1974, the Water Industry Act 1991, the Clear Air Act 1993, and the Radioactive Substances Act 1993.

Limiting the liability of directors

Section 310 of the Companies Act 1985 prohibits the exclusion of liability of directors but s 310(3) makes it possible to provide insurance for directors.

Section 727 of the Companies Act 1985 allows the court to relieve directors of liability where it feels they have acted honestly and reasonably and ought in all the circumstances to be excused in whole or in part. It has been held, however, that this relief does not extend to s 214 of the Insolvency Act (see *Re Produce Marketing* (1989)).

Directors may be able to rely on 'Directors and Officers Insurance' ('D&O' Insurance) if the company has provided such insurance cover. In February 1996 the Law Commission considered the possible imposition of compulsory D&O cover.

Insider dealing

The Criminal Justice Act 1993, Part 5 and Schedule 1 of that Act, deal with insider dealing following the EC Directive on Insider Dealing (89/592).

The scheme of the legislation is to focus on criminal sanctions with no civil remedy. There is no insider trading agency and in general the law only applies to quoted companies. The enforcement is haphazard. The maximum penalty on indictment is seven years' imprisonment plus an unlimited fine.

The company secretary

The role of the company secretary has altered enormously from the days of *Barnett Hoares & Company v South London Tramways Company* (1887), when the company secretary was described by Lord Esher MR, as a 'mere servant'. In 1971 the Court of Appeal, considering the company secretary in *Panorama Developments (Guildford) Ltd v Fidelis Furnishing Fabrics Ltd*, considered the company secretary 'a much more important person', *per* Lord Denning MR.

The company secretary is, today, one of the principal officers of the company. He is the agent through whom much of the company's administrative work is done. Indeed, when making contracts on behalf of the company, it is advisable for the secretary to ensure he does so as agent of the company to avoid any personal liability. The company secretary owes fiduciary duties similar to directors (see *Re Morvah Consols Tin Mining Company* (1876)).

The company secretary has many responsibilities. These include:

- preparation and keeping of minutes (s 382 of the Companies Act 1985);
- dealing with share transfers and issuing share and debenture certificates;
- keeping and maintaining the register of members and debenture-holders (s 352 and s 190 of the Companies Act 1985);
- keeping and maintaining the register of directors and secretary (s 288 of the Companies Act 1985);
- the registration of charges and the maintaining of the company's register of charges (s 399 and s 407 of the Companies Act 1985);
- keeping and maintaining the register of directors' share interests (s 325 of the Companies Act 1985);
- keeping of records of directors' service contracts (s 318 of the Companies Act 1985);
- the collation of directors' interests that have to be disclosed (s 232 and Schedule 6 of the Companies Act 1985);
- keeping and maintaining the register of material share interests (s 211 of the Companies Act 1985);
- sending notices of meetings, copies of accounts etc;
- keeping the company's constitution up to date;
- preparation and submission of the annual return (ss 363–65 of the Companies Act 1985);
- filing of numerous returns and documents;
- preparation of numerous returns required by government departments;
- witnessing documents, together with a director;
- payment of dividends and the preparation of dividend warrants.

It may be that other duties fall upon the company secretary as well. Matters such as employment issues, dealing with the accountants, obtaining legal advice from solicitors and dealing with the Stock Exchange, if this is appropriate.

In a public company s 286 of the Companies Act 1985 requires the company secretary to have a recognised professional qualification. It is the duty of the directors of a public company to take all reasonable steps to ensure that this is the case.

Auditors

Every company must appoint auditors, except companies which are dormant and private companies which are exempt from the audit requirement (s 384 of the Companies Act 1985).

An auditor may be removed by ordinary resolution of the company (s 391 of the Companies Act 1985).

In the case of removal of an auditor, however, special notice must be served. The auditor is entitled to make written representations which are to be circulated to members of the company. The auditor retains a right to compensation for breach of contract.

Note – the written resolution procedure cannot be used for the removal of auditors.

An auditor may resign from office under s 392 of the Companies Act 1985. He must, at the time of resigning, also deposit a statement setting out any circumstances connected with his resignation from office, which he considers should be brought to the attention of the company's members or creditors, or a statement that there are no such circumstances. If there are circumstances which the auditor wishes to bring to the attention of the company, the company must, within 14 days of the deposit of the statement, send copies to the people entitled to copies of the accounts (basically members and debentureholders), or if it considers it contains defamatory matter, apply to the court to ask that the matter should not be circulated. When an auditor does deposit a statement of circumstances, which he wishes to bring to the attention of members or creditors, he may deposit a requisition with the statement requiring the company to call an extraordinary general meeting (s 392A of the Companies Act 1985).

The auditor who is removed, or who has resigned, is still entitled to notice of the general meeting at which it is proposed to fill the vacancy that he is creating (s 391(4) of the Companies Act 1985 and s 392A(8) of the Companies Act 1985).

Remuneration of auditors

Where auditors are appointed by the general meeting, the remuneration should be decided by the general meeting (s 390A(1) of the Companies Act 1985). If the auditors are appointed by the company's directors, they should fix the remuneration, and if by the Secretary of State, where there has been default, he should do so (s 390A(2) of the Companies Act 1985).

Qualification of auditors

Section 289 of the Companies Act 1985 sets out the recognised bodies for the purposes of qualification as a company's auditor. The recognised bodies in the United Kingdom are:
- the Institute of Chartered Accountants in England and Wales;
- the Institute of Chartered Accountants in Scotland;
- the Association of Certified Accountants;
- the Association of Authorised Public Accountants;
- the Institute of Chartered Accountants in Ireland.

The Secretary of State may recognise similar qualifications obtained outside of the United Kingdom for these purposes.

Auditors' duties

The auditors should audit the company's accounts (s 236 of the Companies Act 1985).

In conducting the audit, an auditor is obliged to take a much stricter approach, compared with former days, to his client, physically checking the stock, advising of any unsatisfactory practice, and scrupulously following up any suspicious circumstances.

His best protection is professional insurance. A clear unequivocal letter of appointment from his client is also desirable. It will remind him of what he has agreed to do.

He should be aware of giving ad hoc advice. If he does so, he should stress that it is provisional and not to be relied upon. Even here, the extent to which he can disclaim liability is limited by the Unfair Contract Terms Act 1977.

An auditor's basic duties have been lucidly and uncontroversially outlined by Lord Denning. First, the auditors should verify the arithmetical accuracy of the accounts and the proper vouching of entries in the books.

Secondly, the auditor should make checks to test whether the accounts mask errors or even dishonesty.

Thirdly, the auditor should report on whether the accounts give to the shareholders reliable information respecting the true financial position of the company (*per* Lord Denning in *Fomento (Sterling Area) Ltd v Selsdon Fountain Pen Company Limited* (1958)).

Auditors' liability

The starting point of any survey of auditors' liability is the famous *dictum* of Lopes LJ in *Re Kingston Cotton Mill* (1896), that 'an auditor is not bound to be a detective ... he is a watchdog but not a bloodhound'. The auditors in this case had taken on trust a management assessment of the amount of yarn in stock, failing to make physical checks themselves. The assessments were frauds which had been perpetrated by a manager to make the company appear to flourish by exaggerating the quantity and value of cotton and yarn in his company's mills.

An auditor is required to investigate suspicious circumstances. In *Re Thomas Gerrard* (1967), Pennycuick J noted that 'the standards of reasonable care and skill are from the expert evidence more exacting than those which prevailed in 1896' (*Re Kingston Cotton Mill*). Here, in addition to an overstatement of stock, there had been fraudulent practice in changing invoice dates to make it appear that clients owed money within the accounting period when in fact it was due outside of it, and to make it appear that suppliers were not yet owed money for goods when such liability did exist. Pennycuick J held Kevans, the auditors, liable.

Liability may arise in contract. The auditor will be liable for failing to perform properly what he has undertaken to do. The other party to the contract – the company – is the only person who can sue the auditor under this head of liability.

An auditor may be liable in negligence to his client or in the tort of negligent misstatement to third parties. Formerly it was the law that there was no duty owed to third parties to exercise care in drawing up accounts. In *Candler v Crane Christmas & Company* (1951), the auditors prepared inaccurate accounts which were relied upon by the plaintiff as the basis for investing money in the company. The majority of the Court of Appeal refused to allow an action in such circumstances.

However, in an historic decision in *Hedley Byrne v Heller* (1964), the House of Lords overruled the *Candler* decision. Liability could henceforth arise where an auditor knew, or ought to have known, that his report would be relied upon and he was negligent in preparing it.

In *JEB Fasteners v Marks Bloom & Company (a firm)* (1981) it was held that the defendants who audited the accounts owed a duty of care to the plaintiffs who relied upon them in purchasing the business. The defendants escaped liability on another ground.

In *Caparo Industries plc v Dickman and others* (1990), the House of Lords held that liability was restricted to cases where the auditor knows of the user and the use to which he will put the information. Such a case arose in *Barings plc v Coopers and Lybrand* (1996) where the Court of Appeal held that Barings had a right of action against Coopers and Lybrand since they knew that their report on Barings Securities Ltd (a subsidiary) were to be relied upon by Barings plc, the holding company.

An auditor may also be liable in a winding up for misfeasance or breach of duty to the company (s 212 of the Insolvency Act 1986). Where this occurs, the court will order whatever compensation it thinks fit.

5 Company meetings and the protection of the company's shareholders

> You should be familiar with the following areas:
>
> - the different types of company meeting and the different methods of calling meetings
> - the conduct of a meeting including the different types of resolution
> - company investigations and the possible consequences of an investigation
> - the rule in *Foss v Harbottle* and exceptions to it
> - the statutory remedy for unfairly prejudiced members
> - just and equitable winding up

Introduction

Minority protection is of fundamental importance and is therefore considered in depth.

Meetings

Annual general meetings

Section 366 of the Companies Act 1985 requires an annual general meeting in every calendar year. Section 366(A) permits private companies to dispense with the holding of an annual general meeting.

Section 367 permits the Secretary of State to call an annual general meeting in default.

Extraordinary general meetings

These may be called as follows:
- directors (see Table A, Article 37 for example);
- request of members – s 368 of the Companies Act 1985 allows two or more members holdings 10% of the shareholding to requisition the calling of an extraordinary general meeting;
- members – s 370(3) of the Companies Act 1985 applies in the event that there is no other provision for the calling of extraordinary general meetings in the articles. This allows two or more members holding 10% of the shares to call a meeting directly;
- the court – s 371 of the Companies Act 1985 gives a residual right to the court to call an extraordinary general meeting. This is often done where there is a problem in obtaining a quorum, see eg *Re Sticky Fingers Restaurant Ltd* (1992);
- resigning auditors – s 392(A) of the Companies Act 1985;
- a serious loss of capital in a public company – s 142 of the Companies Act 1985.

The conduct of meetings

Notice

(i) *Length of notice* – the length of notice for an annual general meeting is 21 days. For extraordinary general meetings the length of notice is 14 days for a limited company and seven days for an unlimited company. However, if a special resolution is to be proposed, 21 days' notice is required.
- Section 369(3) of the Companies Act 1985 allows meetings to be called on short notice in certain circumstances.

(ii) *Content* – the notice must clearly set out the date, time and place of the meeting. It should also set out the text of any resolution to be proposed.
•If the meeting is an annual general meeting, the notice must say so. The right to appoint a proxy and that the proxy need not be a member should always be set out.

(iii) *Serving the notice* – s 370(2) of the Companies Act 1985 provides that the notice should be served in the manner required by Table A. This applies if there is no contrary provision.
•Table A, Article 39, provides that the accidental omission to serve the notice does not invalidate the meeting.
•Table A, Article 116, provides that a notice may be given by the company

to a person entitled to a share as the result of death or bankruptcy of a member, by sending or delivering the notice in any manner prescribed by the Articles, or until notice of an address has been given, by serving it in the manner in which it would have been served had the death or bankruptcy not occurred.
• Table A, Article 38, provides that notice should be served on members, directors and the company's auditors.

The chairman

Table A, Article 42, provides that the chairman of the board of directors is to act as chairman, or some other nominated director may do so.

The chairman is responsible for taking the meeting through the agenda, putting matters to the vote and keeping order, see eg *John v Rees* (1969).

The chairman's declaration of the result of any vote is conclusive in the absence of fraud or obvious mistake, see *Re Caratal (New) Mines Ltd* (1902).

Quorum

Section 370(4) provides for a quorum of two members unless the company's articles provide otherwise. Note the problem of meetings of one person, see *Sharpe v Dawes* (1876), *Re Sanitary Carbon Company* (1877), and *Re London Flats Ltd* (1969).

Note – sometimes meetings may be held with one member:
* a class meeting of one where there is only one in the class, see eg *East v Bennett Bros* (1911);
* private companies with only one member, the 12th EC Directive on Company Law permits this;
* an annual general meeting ordered by the Secretary of State fixing the quorum at one under s 367 of the Companies Act 1985;
* a meeting ordered by the court under s 371 of the Companies Act 1985 where the quorum is fixed at one (see *Re Sticky Fingers Restaurant Ltd* (1992) above).

It would appear that meetings can be held validly even though the members are not all in each other's physical presence if there is an effective audio/visual link (see *Byng v London Life Association Ltd* (1990)).

Special notice

Special notice is defined in s 379 of the Companies Act 1985. It is 28 days' notice of the resolution given to the company by a member. It is needed in three, and only three, situations:
- the removal of a director under s 303 of the Companies Act 1985;
- the appointment or reappointment of a director aged 70 or above in a public company or in a private company which is a subsidiary of a public company under s 293 of the Companies Act 1985;
- the removal of an auditor under s 391A of the Companies Act 1985.

Resolutions

There are various types of resolution:

Extraordinary resolution

This is one passed by a majority of at least 75% of those voting after 14 days' notice (s 378(1) of the Companies Act 1985), eg a resolution to wind up where a company cannot pay its debts (s 84(1) of the Insolvency Act 1986).

Special resolution

This is one passed by a majority of at least 75% of those voting after 21 days' notice (s 378(2) of the Companies Act 1985), eg a resolution to change the company's articles of association (s 9 of the Companies Act 1985).

Ordinary resolution

This is not defined in the Act. It is passed by a simple majority of those voting. It will usually involve 14 days' notice. It is used extensively, eg a resolution to increase a company's authorised share capital (s 121 of the Companies Act 1985), a resolution to remove a director (s 303 of the Companies Act 1985), and a resolution to remove the auditors (s 391A of the Companies Act 1985).

Written resolution

The Companies Act 1989 introduced a new procedure whereby a private company may act by unanimous written resolution without the need for a meeting. There are a few situations where the procedures cannot be used, eg the removal of a director and the removal of the auditors.

On occasion the courts have been willing to apply 'the assent principle' to unanimity where there has been no meeting regardless of the type of company involved, see eg *Re Express Engineering Works Ltd* (1920).

Elective resolution

The Companies Act 1989 introduced a new regime relaxing certain formalities for private companies. Private companies may, by unanimous resolution, whether in writing or passed at a meeting, achieve the following:

- dispense with the annual laying of accounts and reports (s 252 of the Companies Act 1985);
- dispense with the holding of an annual general meeting (s 366A of the Companies Act 1985);
- dispense with the annual appointment of auditors (s 386 of the Companies Act 1985);
- reduce the majority required to give consent to the holding of an extraordinary general meeting at short notice from 95% to 90% (s 369(4) and s 378(3) of the Companies Act 1985);
- grant the power to the directors to issue shares or debentures without a time limit (s 80A of the Companies Act 1985).

Votes

Votes are first conducted on a show of hands with one vote per member, proxies not voting unless the articles so provide. A poll may be demanded by any five members (here proxies count), or 10% of the voting rights (s 373 of the Companies Act 1985). A decision on a poll will override the decision on the show of hands.

Proxies

Every member has the right to appoint a proxy and that proxy need not be a member (s 372 of the Companies Act 1985). In a private company, a proxy can speak at a meeting.

A provision requiring the instrument appointing the proxy to be received by the company more than 48 hours before the meeting is void.

Adjournment

Table A provides for adjournment of a meeting if required by the members. At common law there is a power to adjourn if there is disorder or if there is a problem accommodating all those turning up.

Minutes

Companies must keep minutes of all general meetings (s 382 of the Companies Act 1985).

Company investigations

Production of documents

The DTI may require a company to produce documents (s 447 of the Companies Act 1985). This power is reinforced by a power of entry and search (s 448 of the Companies Act 1985). This is often the precursor to an investigation.

Investigation of affairs of a company

Section 431 of the Act provides that the Secretary of State may appoint inspectors to investigate a company's affairs on the application of not less than 200 members or of members holding not less than 10% of the issued shares or, in the case of a company without share capital, one-fifth of the members or the company itself. The application must be supported by such evidence as the Secretary of State may require.

Section 432 provides that the Secretary of State must appoint inspectors if so ordered by the court and may do so if there are circumstances suggesting:

• that the company's affairs are being or have been conducted with intent to defraud creditors or otherwise for a fraudulent or unlawful purpose or in a manner which is unfairly prejudicial to some part of the members; or

- that an actual or proposed act or omission is or would be so prejudicial or that the company was formed for any fraudulent or unlawful purpose;
- that persons connected with the company's formation or management have been guilty of fraud, misfeasance or other misconduct toward the company or its members; or
- the company's members have not been given all the information with respect to the company's affairs which they might reasonably expect (s 432(2) of the Companies Act 1985).

Investigation of ownership or control

Section 442 of the Companies Act 1985 enables the Secretary of State to appoint inspectors if he feels there is good reason to investigate the ownership or control of a company. He must order an investigation if an application is made by 200 or more members or by members holding 10% or more of the company's issued shares.

Investigation of directors' share dealings

Section 446 of the Companies Act 1985 provides that the Secretary of State may appoint inspectors if he feels there has been a contravention of s 323 (prohibition on directors dealing in share options) or of s 324 (disclosure of directors' shareholdings).

Other companies in the group

In each of the above instances, the inspector may investigate any other company in the group.

Investigation into insider dealing

If the Secretary of State suspects breaches of the insider dealing legislation, he may appoint inspectors under s 177 of the Financial Services Act 1986.

Consequences of an inspection

An inspection may lead to:

- a petition by the Secretary of State under s 124(4) of the Insolvency Act 1986 to wind the company up on the just and equitable ground;
- civil proceedings being brought by the Secretary of State in the name of the company (s 438 of the Companies Act 1985);
- a petition being brought by the Secretary of State on the basis of unfair prejudice to the members (s 460 of the Companies Act 1985);
- an application for a disqualification order against individual directors or shadow directors (s 8 of the Company Directors' Disqualification Act 1986).

Minority protection

There are two principal areas that need to be looked at in the context of minority protection. The first of these is the rule in *Foss v Harbottle* (1843) and the exceptions to that rule. Secondly, the statutory remedy for members who are unfairly prejudiced in the conduct of the company's affairs will be examined.

The historic decision in *Foss v Harbottle* concerned park land in Moss Side, Manchester, which was then a leafy suburb of the city. Businessmen in the city had grouped together to purchase land to dedicate to the then heiress to the throne, Princess Victoria. The park opened to great rejoicing. Difficulties soon followed. Some of the company's members alleged that certain directors had misapplied company property. It was alleged that the directors had taken, for themselves, out of the monies of the company, a price exceeding the value of the land. Wigwram VC held that the action could not proceed. The wrong had not been done to individual shareholders but to the company, if a wrong existed at all. The judge said:

The Victoria Park Company is an incorporated body, and the conduct with which the defendants are charged in this suit is an injury not to the plaintiffs exclusively; it is an injury to the whole corporation by individuals whom the corporation entrusted with powers to be exercised only for the good of the corporation.

This principle – the rule in *Foss v Harbottle* – has acted like a dead hand on minority protection in British company law. The rule may be justified. A company may ratify what has been done and that might, therefore, make litigation pointless. Another possible ground on which the decision may be justified is that it prevents a multiplicity of actions. This second objection may be overcome by permitting a class action on behalf of all of the shareholders wronged.

The principle in *Foss v Harbottle* was applied in *McDougall v Gardiner* (1875). In this case, some shareholders complained that the company, the Silver Mining Company Ltd, had failed to hold special general meetings. The Court of Appeal held that the company was the proper plaintiff to bring an action against those responsible for the failure.

There are certain established exceptions to the principle in *Foss v Harbottle*. The areas of exception are set out with clarity in the judgment of Jenkins LJ in *Edwards v Halliwell* (1950):

- An *ultra vires* act
  If the complaint by a shareholder is that the company has engaged in an *ultra vires* activity, traditionally, a minority action as an exception to *Foss v Harbottle* has been permitted. It used to be the case that *ultra vires* activities could not be ratified. Thus, in *Parke v Daily News Ltd* (1962), the single shareholder was able to bring an action to restrain the company from giving payments to employees in excess of those to which they were entitled by law or under contract. Similarly, in *Simpson v Westminster Palace Hotel* (1868), a shareholder was able to bring an action complaining that the company was acting *ultra vires* in proposing to use hotel rooms for offices. Recently the Companies Act 1989 has amended the law on *ultra vires*. It is now only possible to restrain an *ultra vires* activity in advance of a transaction being entered into (see s 35(2) of the Companies Act 1985). It is thus now the position that a single shareholder may bring an action to restrain a proposed *ultra vires* act. In relation to concluded acts that are *ultra vires*, it will usually be the case that the transaction is valid.

- The special majorities exception
  Where a company's constitution stipulates that a special majority is needed before a particular course of action can be accomplished, then if the company seeks to flout this without obtaining the required majority, a single shareholder may maintain an action as an exception to *Foss v Harbottle*. This was the case in *Edwards v Halliwell* itself. In fact, the case concerns a point of trade union law rather than company law but in this area the principles are identical. The National Union of Vehicle Builders had a provision in its rule book that provided that the members' subscriptions could only be increased by a ballot vote of members resulting in a two-thirds majority for the proposal. In contravention of this provision, a dele-

gate meeting purported to increase the subscription. A branch of the union objected. The Court of Appeal held that the rule in *Foss v Harbottle* could not be relied upon in this instance. It was a recognised exception to the rule that where a particular majority was required and that majority had not been obtained, then an individual member may bring an action as an exception to *Foss v Harbottle*.

* The personal rights exception
Where a company denies a member rights that are set out in the company's constitution, the member may maintain an action as an exception to *Foss v Harbottle*. Thus, in *Pender v Lushington* (1877), a shareholder was able to enforce his right and that of other shareholders that they should be able to cast their votes. In *Wood v Odessa Waterworks* (1889), a shareholder was able to enforce his right to a dividend to be paid in cash rather than in property where this was provided for under the company's articles.

* Fraud by those in control
The most important exception to the rule in *Foss v Harbottle* is where fraud has been perpetrated by those in control of the company. It seems from *Prudential Assurance v Newman Industries* (1980) that 'those in control' may mean those in day to day management control who might not have a controlling majority of votes in general meeting.
Fraud may never be ratified. The objection to a single member bringing an action on behalf of all members where the conduct complained of may be subsequently ratified does not therefore apply in this instance. Thus in *Cooke v Deeks* (1916), a Privy Council case on appeal from Ontario, a shareholder was able to bring an action under this head complaining that directors had diverted corporate opportunities away from the company to themselves personally. The exception is limited to cases of fraud. It does not apply in cases of negligence, eg *Pavlides v Jensen* (1956) where the complaint was that the directors had been negligent in selling an asbestos mine in Cyprus at an undervaluation. Similarly, in *Heyting v Dupont* (1964), the complaint was one of negligence not one of fraud and so the action could not proceed.
A special case is that of *Daniels v Daniels* (1978). In this case, the complaint was framed as one of negligence. It concerned a purchase by a director of property from the company for £4,250 and its subsequent re-sale for some £120,000 by the director concerned. Templeman J allowed the action to proceed. He said that mere negligence is one thing but negligence with such a massive profit to the

negligent party is quite another thing. Clearly, the decision is exceptional and turned on its particular facts.

Another unusual case is *Estmanco (Kilner House) Ltd v Greater London Council* (1982). In this case, the shareholders in the company had no voting rights. They were leaseholders in a block of flats. Voting control was vested in the local authority. The management agreement provided that the council would use its best endeavours to sell the flats. Subsequently there was a change of political control of the council. The council decided not to proceed with sale of the properties. One of the leaseholders, who was a member of the company, sought to proceed with this action. Megarry VC held that this case fell within 'the fraud on the minority' exception.

It has been argued that of these four apparent exceptions to the rule in *Foss v Harbottle*, only the fourth is a true exception. The other three instances are said to be examples of the company violating its constitution, injuring the member who may then pursue a claim against the company (see, for example, Harry Rajak, *A Sourcebook of Company Law*, Jordans, p 606).

The statutory remedy

Of far more importance in practice to the rule in *Foss v Harbottle* and its exceptions is the statutory remedy. The difficulties with *Foss v Harbottle* led to the introduction of a statutory remedy in s 210 of the Companies Act 1948. This followed the report of the Committee on Company Law Amendment (the Cohen Committee of 1945). The Committee urged:

... there be a new section under which, on a shareholder's petition, the court, if satisfied that a minority of the shareholders is being oppressed and that a winding up order would not do justice to the minority, should be empowered, instead of making a winding up order, to make such other order, including an order for the purchase by the majority of the shares of the minority at a price to be fixed by the court as to the court may seem just.

There were difficulties with s 210 of the Companies Act 1948. These difficulties were highlighted by the Jenkins Committee in 1962. The drawbacks were as follows:
- An order could only be made if the facts could be the basis of a winding up order on the just and equitable grounds. This meant that the section was closely allied to the rules relating to winding up.
- A single act was insufficient to justify a petition under s 210. A course of conduct had to be shown.

- The petitioner had to show that the conduct was oppressive. This meant 'burdensome, harsh and wrongful' (see *Scottish CWS v Mayer* (1959)).
- A petition could not be based on omissions or threatened future conduct.
- There was some doubt as to whether the section could be used by personal representatives. It was, however, stated in *Re Jermyn Street Turkish Baths Ltd* (1971) by Plowman J that personal representatives could petition.

Since difficulties were encountered with s 210 of the Companies Act 1948 which was only used successfully in two cases, the law was amended. Section 75 of the Companies Act 1980 was introduced. The remedy in s 75 answered many of the difficulties of the old section. The link with winding up was swept away. A single act or an omission or threatened future conduct can be the basis for a petition. Personal representatives can now sue. Most importantly, the new remedy applies in cases of 'unfair prejudice'. This is clearly a far wider remedy than a remedy for oppression. Section 75 provided that the remedy was available to 'some part of the company's members'. This led to difficulties since it was interpreted in some cases as meaning that the remedy could not be used if all of the membership was unfairly prejudiced. This had been the view of Vinelott J in *Re Carrington Viyella plc* (1983), for example. The Companies Act 1989 duly amended the section to make it clear that the remedy is available even if all of the members of the company are prejudiced. The section reads as follows:

A member of a company may apply to the court by petition for an order under this part on the ground that the company's affairs are being or have been conducted in a manner which is unfairly prejudicial to the interests of its members generally or of some part of its members (including at least himself) or that any actual or proposed act or omission of the company (including an act or omission on its behalf) is or would be so prejudicial.

The most frequent cause for complaint is exclusion from management – generally in a quasi-partnership type company like the one in *Ebrahimi v Westbourne Galleries Ltd* (1973). Under the old law, it was necessary that oppression had been suffered qua member. This was a narrow interpretation of the section. Initially it seemed that this narrow interpretation would be applied to the amended remedy as well. In *Re a company 004475* (1983), Lord Grantchester QC held that prejudice had to be suffered qua member in the narrow sense. In an earlier unreported case, however, Slade J had allowed a remedy for exclusion from management in *Re Bovey Hotel Ventures Ltd* (1981). Petitions have been successful on the basis of exclusion in a number of cases (see, for example, *Re Bird Precision Bellows Ltd* (1985), *Re a company No 00477 of 1986* (1986)). In other cases, petitions on the basis of exclusion from management have failed. Where they have failed, however, this has been because of the facts. Thus, exclusion from management failed in *Re a company No 003843 of 1986* (1987) where the company had not been established on a quasi-partnership basis. Exclusion from management also failed in *Re a company No 004377 of 1986 (XYZ Ltd)* (1986) where the company's constitution made provision for such an eventuality. It may also be that a remedy is denied where the exclusion was justified because of the petitioner's conduct (see, for example, *Re R A Noble & Sons (Clothing) Ltd* (1983)).

There have been many other petitions where particular conduct has been recognised as capable of being unfairly prejudicial:

- Allotting shares in breach of pre-emption rights
  Re DR Chemicals Ltd (1989).

- Convening a meeting of the company for a date unreasonably into the distant future
  McGuinness & Another, Petitioners (1988).

- Failure to pay proper dividends
  Re Sam Weller & Sons Ltd (1989).

- Diverting business away from the company
  Re Cumana (1986).

- Making a rights issue in certain circumstances
  Re a company No 007623 of 1984 (1986).

- Providing misleading information to a company's shareholders
  Re a company No 008699 of 1985 (1986).

- A proposal to sell the company's business at a substantial under-valuation to connected persons
  Re Posgate & Denby (Agencies) Ltd (1987).

- Using the company's assets for the benefit of the company's controlling shareholders and family
  Re Elgindata (1991).

The section may be used by members or personal representatives of members.

It is not necessary that a person should come to court with clean hands (see *Re London School of Electronics* (1986)). However, if a petitioner has to some extent brought the relevant conduct upon himself, this may be material in deciding whether the prejudice is unfair and it may also be relevant in deciding what remedy if any should be available to the petitioner.

The question of unfair prejudice is an objective one. It is not necessary to show that the petitioner acted maliciously (see *Re RA Noble & Sons (Clothing) Ltd* (1983)).

Remedies

The court has the power to award whatever relief it considers fit (s 461(1) of the Companies Act 1985). It may make an order regulating the company's affairs or restricting the company from acting in a particular way. It may order the company to do something or it may order civil proceedings to be brought in the name of the company. A common remedy is where the court orders the purchase of a petitioner's shares. On occasion, it may even be an order that the respondent sells his shares to the petitioner. This occurred in *Re Bovey Hotel Ventures Ltd* (1981).

Where an order is made for the purchase of shares, problems of valuation arise. There is no rule in s 461 regarding a valuation of shares.

Generally, where a minority shareholding is sold, an element of discount is applied; so, for example, if 10% of the shares are to be sold, this would not represent a 10% value of the company's net assets. However, in relation to s 459, the sale is a forced sale. As Vinelott J said in *Re Bird Precision Bellows Ltd* (1984) at first instance:

... on the assumption that the unfair prejudice has made it no longer tolerable for him to retain his interest in the company, the sale of his shares will inevitably be his only practical way out short of a winding up. In that case it seems to me that it would not merely not be fair, but most unfair that he should be bought out on a fictional basis applicable to a free election to sell his shares in accordance with the company's articles of association, or indeed on any other basis which involved a discounted price. In my judgment the correct course would be to fix the price pro rata according to the value of the shares as a whole without any discount, as being the only fair method of compensating an unwilling vendor of the equivalent of a partnership share.

Another moot point is on what date the shares should be valued.

Again, there is no fixed rule to apply. If the petitioner refused a reasonable offer for his shares, the date of valuation may well be the date of the hearing (see *Re a company No 992567 of 1982* (1983)).

On the other hand, if a fair offer is not made and the conduct of the majority causes the value of the company's shares to fall, the court may order a valuation at the date that the unreasonable conduct began (see *Re O C (Transport) Services Ltd* (1984)). This does indeed seem to be the most logical date for valuing the shares.

Just and equitable winding up

It may in some ways seem incongruous to consider winding up in the context of minority remedies. In truth, however, the just and equitable ground for winding up is a member's remedy. It is important to remember this in the context of a possible essay or, indeed, a problem question relating to remedies for members.

A company may be wound up by the court if the court is of the opinion that it is just and equitable that the company should be wound up (s 122(1)(g) of the Insolvency Act 1986). Before the advent of ss 459–61 of the Companies Act 1985, just and equitable winding up was sometimes the only possible remedy for a disenchanted minority shareholder. The difficulties of framing an action as an exception to *Foss v Harbottle* have already been noted. Since the advent of ss 459–61, use of just and equitable winding up has been less common. Indeed, s 125(2) of the Insolvency Act 1986 provides that if the court is of the opinion that there is some other remedy that is available to the petitioners and that they are acting unreasonably in seeking to have the company wound up instead of pursuing that other remedy, then the court should refuse the petition. Yet in *Virdi v Abbey Leisure Ltd* (1989), the Court of Appeal considered that where a minority sought a winding up order, rather than utilising a mechanism in the articles for selling the shares, that this was not acting unreasonably. The Court of Appeal, reversing Hoffmann J at first instance, considered that the minority might legitimately object to the mode of valuation in assessing the value of the shares and prefer to leave it to the marketplace.

The most famous case in relation to just and equitable winding up is undoubtedly *Ebrahimi v Westbourne Galleries Ltd* (1973). The House of Lords in this case stated unequivocally that the categories of conduct justifying winding up on the just and equitable ground are not closed. It is attempted here to classify some of the circumstances where just and equitable winding up may be awarded.

In *Ebrahimi* itself the ground was exclusion from management in a quasi-partnership company. In *Re A&BC Chewing Gum Ltd* (1975), the ground of the petition was similar. In *Tay Bok Choon v Tahansan Sdn Bhd* (1987), the shareholder who was excluded from management in a small company was able to petition for just and equitable winding up in a similar way in Malaysia.

Another ground on which just and equitable winding up may be awarded is if the purpose for which the company was formed can no longer be achieved (sometimes called the destruction of the substratum of the company). This was the successful ground in *Re German Date Coffee Co* (1882). Here the company had been formed to obtain a German patent to manufacture coffee from dates. The application for the patent was refused. A petition to wind the company up was granted. Such a petition can only succeed, however, if all of the company's main purposes are no longer capable of achievement. Thus, in *Re Kitson & Co Ltd* (1946), where the company had other activities that could be accomplished in addition to the engineering business which had ceased, a petition to wind the company up was not granted.

If there is deadlock within the company and that deadlock cannot be broken, then a petition to wind the company up will be successful. In *Re Yenidje Tobacco Co Ltd* (1916), the company had two shareholders with an equal number of shares. They were each directors. They could not agree on how the company should be run. There was no provision for breaking the deadlock and a petition to wind the company up on the just and equitable ground was therefore successful.

A further ground for a just and equitable winding up petition and one which has found favour with the courts is lack of honesty of the directors. In *Re Bleriot Manufacturing Aircraft Co* (1916), the court held that where directors had misappropriated company property a winding up order could be made. In *Loch v John Blackwood Ltd* (1924), a Privy Council decision on appeal from the Court of Appeal of the West Indies (Barbados), where directors had failed to supply full information to the company's members, a petition was successful. A more recent instance is to be found in *Re Lundie Bros Ltd* (1965) where directors were running the business as if it were their own personal property.

There are, therefore, certain categories of conduct which are clearly established as giving rise to the ability to present a petition to wind the company up on the just and equitable ground.

You are advised to ensure in answering any question, whether it be essay or problem question, to consider the full range of shareholder protection that might be available. Exceptions to *Foss v Harbottle* are less important in practice than formerly. However, they may well still rear their head in the examination room! Sections 459–61 are extremely important. Not only will they crop up in essay and problem questions specifically designed to test a candidate's knowledge on these areas, but they must be borne in mind in answering any question on company law as disgruntled shareholders may feature in any problem question. Do not forget just and equitable winding up as a shareholder's remedy either. In addition, there may be other areas which involve shareholder protection which you may be able to invoke. For example, minorities are able to require company meetings to be called; at meetings they may require a poll; minorities may be able to force a company investigation etc. In short, the whole question of shareholder protection permeates the entire Companies Act and you should seek to display a breadth of knowledge in answering examination questions involving shareholder protection.

6 The company in trouble, reconstructions and take-overs

You should be familiar with the following areas:

- the nature of loan stock (debentures)
- the different types of charges and the procedure for the registration of charges
- receivership
- voluntary arrangements
- administration
- the different types of liquidation and the conduct of a liquidation
- fraudulent and wrongful trading
- the different procedures for take-overs, reconstructions and amalgamations

Introduction

This chapter covers a great deal of ground. Wrongful trading is important and topical, and knowledge of priorities in a winding up is of great importance. Other areas are also covered. Take-overs however, are only dealt with in outline.

Loan stock (debentures)

Any form of borrowing by a company is technically a debenture (s 744 of the Companies Act 1985). In practice, the term debenture is generally used to describe a secured borrowing and debentures are generally subject to the law of mortgages. The only exception to this principle is that a debenture need not be redeemable at a set date (see s 193 of the Companies Act 1985).

Where a company borrows money from a bank, there may be a single debenture. In other situations, particularly in relation to quoted companies, there may be an issue of debenture stock similar to an issue of shares. In such a situation, there will be a debenture trust deed. This will set out the terms of the loan. There will be a trustee who will act on behalf of all debentureholders.

Debentures compared with shares

Debentures and shares have certain similarities. The transfer procedure is similar. Where debentures are issued to the public, the same principles apply as in relation to an issue of shares pertaining to a prospectus or listing particulars.

There are, however, certain key distinctions. A debentureholder is a creditor of a company whereas a shareholder is a member. The company is free to purchase its own debentures whereas there are strict rules governing purchase by a company of its own shares.

Debentures may be issued at a discount whilst shares cannot be issued at a discount (see s 100 of the Companies Act 1985).

Interest on a debenture is due as a debt and may be paid out of capital; a dividend on a share can only be paid out of profits.

Charges

It has been noted that in practice a debenture is a secured loan. A debenture may be secured in one of two ways. It may be secured by a fixed charge. A fixed charge is similar to an ordinary mortgage and is effective from the time of its creation. It may also be secured by a floating charge. The floating charge is unique to company law. It is created over the whole of the company's assets and undertakings. It is not effective until something happens to cause the charge to crystallise. It is beneficial to the company in that it enables the company to borrow money and to mortgage back to the lender of the money all of the company's assets and undertakings including its work in progress, finished products and raw materials. The nature of a floating charge was described in *Re Yorkshire Woolcombers Association Ltd* (1904). The House of Lords there stated that the floating charge is over a class of assets present and future; the company can continue to do business and to dispose of its assets in the course of that business and the assets within the class of assets subject to the floating charge will fluctuate and change as the company trades.

A floating charge will crystallise in certain circumstances:

- if the company goes into liquidation;
- if a receiver is appointed, either by the court or under the terms of the debenture;
- if there is cessation of the company's trade or business;
- if an event occurs which, by the terms of the debenture, causes the floating charge to crystallise.

This last head causes controversy. The question arises as to whether the debenture will automatically crystallise or whether the happening of the event permits the debentureholders to act to bring about crystallisation. *Re Manurewa Transport Ltd* (1971) (New Zealand) held that crystallisation occurs automatically. This was approved *obiter* by Hoffmann J in *Re Brightlife Ltd* (1986).

Section 413 of the Companies Act 1985 permits the Secretary of State to make regulations requiring that notice should be given to the registrar of companies of an event causing automatic crystallisation. In such a situation, the occurrence of such events will not be effective until the required information has been delivered.

Most charges require registration. Categories of charges that have to be registered are set out in s 396 of the Companies Act 1985. The categories include all floating charges and most fixed charges.

The charge must be registered within 21 days of its creation. Failure so to register a charge renders it void. This does not, of course, affect the validity of the debt. If a company acquires property that is already subject to a charge, the obligation to register accrues on the date of its acquisition. The failure to register in such a situation, however, does not render the charge void but merely exposes the officers concerned to liability to a default fine.

Section 400 of the Companies Act 1985 makes provision for late delivery of particulars. In such a situation, if at the time of the delivery the company is unable to pay its debts as they fall due or it becomes unable to do so because of that transaction, then the charge is void against the administrator, liquidator or other person if insolvency proceedings begin before the end of two years in the case of a floating charge in favour of a connected person, one year in the case of a floating charge in favour of an unconnected person and six months in any other case.

When a charge is paid off, a memorandum should be delivered to the registrar of companies to record this event (s 403(1) of the Companies Act 1985).

Priorities amongst charges

Sometimes problems may arise regarding the priority amongst various charges. This may occur where there is an administrative receivership or where there is a liquidation.

The general rule is that fixed charges which are effective from the time of creation have priority over floating charges which only have efficacy from the time of crystallisation.

The only exception to this is that a floating charge which contains a negative pledge provision may have priority over a later fixed charge. This is the principle in *Wilson v Kelland* (1910). At present this type of negative pledge provision is only effective if it is actually known of by the subsequent fixed chargeholder. However, the Companies Act 1985 (amended by the Companies Act 1989) contains a provision to the effect that the Secretary of State for Trade and Industry may require such negative pledge clauses to be recorded in the register at Companies House. Were he to require this type of clause to be registered, then constructive notice of this would apply to subsequent fixed chargeholders.

As between two or more fixed charges over the same property, clearly the first in time has priority. The same principle generally applies where there is a second floating charge over the same property (see *Re Benjamin Cope & Sons Ltd* (1914)). An exception to this, however, is if the first floating charge leaves open the possibility of a second floating charge taking priority over it where the second floating charge is over a specific category of property narrower than the first which would be over the entire assets and undertaking of the company (see *Re Automatic Bottlemakers* (1926)).

In any problem concerning priorities, it is important to bear other factors in mind as well. Where questions of priority arise, the costs (including remuneration) of the administrative receiver or liquidator will always be paid off before fixed and floating charges. Preferential creditors are paid off ahead of the beneficiaries of a floating charge. The categories of preferential creditor are set out in Schedule 6 of the Insolvency Act 1986.

Another important feature to bear in mind is the possibility of a valid reservation of title clause (see *Aluminium Industrie Vaassen BV v*

Romalpa Aluminium Ltd (1976)). Where there is an effective reservation of title clause, this may well mean that property which is on the premises of the company concerned does not come within the control of the administrative receiver or liquidator because it still belongs to the supplier. The examiner is fond of such clauses!

In a similar way, the examiner may slip a lien into the problem question. For example, if the fleet of company cars is out for repair at a garage and the repair work has been done but the cars are still parked on the forecourt of the garage, the liquidator or administrative receiver cannot take control of the cars until he has paid the fees owing to the garage (see *George Barker (Transport) Ltd v Eynon* (1974)).

Receivership

Where a debentureholder seeks to enforce the terms of a debenture where there has been default, the appropriate remedy is generally to secure the appointment of a receiver. If the debentureholder is seeking to enforce a fixed charge, he will appoint a receiver. Such a person need not be a qualified insolvency practitioner. If he is seeking to enforce the terms of a floating charge, then he will seek to appoint an administrative receiver. Such a person must be a qualified insolvency practitioner. Certain professional bodies' members may act as insolvency practitioners. These bodies are:

* The Law Society;
* The Institute of Chartered Accountants in England and Wales;
* The Chartered Association of Certified Accountants;
* The Insolvency Practitioners Association.

Where a person is appointed an administrative receiver, then the appointment will be in writing unless it is by court order. Notice must be given to the registrar of companies (s 409 of the Companies Act 1985).

The person appointed as administrative receiver must notify the company of his appointment and all of the company's creditors so far as their addresses are known to him. Additionally, administrative receivers must ensure there is a statement of their appointment contained in the *London Gazette*.

In every receivership, publicity must be given to the fact that there is a receivership. It must be stated on every invoice, order for goods or business letter issued by or on behalf of the company or the receiver or manager where the company's name appears.

The administrative receiver should seek to take control of the assets subject to the floating charge, realise the assets and pay off the creditors in due order of priority. As has been noted above, preferential creditors must be paid ahead of the beneficiaries of a floating charge.

The administrative receiver will require the directors of the company to produce a statement of affairs of the company setting out the company's assets, debts, liabilities and securities. The administrative receiver should draft his own report which should be sent to the registrar of companies, to any trustees for secured creditors and to all secured creditors for whom he has an address.

In general, similar principles apply in relation to a receiver where there is a fixed charge. In this situation, however, preferential creditors do not enjoy the same priority, and there is no statement of affairs.

When an administrative receiver has completed his task, he may vacate office. He must give notice of this to the registrar of companies. He must also vacate office if he ceases to be qualified as an insolvency practitioner.

Voluntary arrangements

Voluntary arrangements are dealt with in Part 1 of the Insolvency Act 1986. This provides a simple procedure where a company in financial difficulties can enter into a voluntary arrangement with its creditors. It may involve a composition in satisfaction of debts or a scheme of arrangement of the company's affairs.

The voluntary arrangement must be supervised by a 'nominee'. This nominee must be a qualified insolvency practitioner. The nominee should submit a report to the court stating whether in his opinion meetings of the company and of its creditors should be summoned to consider the proposal put to him by directors of the company. The proposal where meetings are called must be approved by three-quarters in value of the creditors and by a simple majority of the members.

Once the proposal for the voluntary arrangement has taken effect, the nominee becomes the supervisor of the composition of the voluntary arrangement.

The arrangement is a valuable one. It was added at the behest of the Cork Committee.

Administration

This is another innovation following the Review Committee on Insolvency Law and Practice – the Cork Report. It makes possible the rescue of a company by placing its management in the hands of an administrator. The administrator must be a qualified insolvency practitioner.

The court may make an order on the application, *inter alia*, of the company or its directors or a creditor or creditors or the supervisor of a voluntary arrangement.

The court has to be satisfied that the company is, or is likely, to become unable to pay its debts and must consider that the making of an order makes one or more of the purposes set out below achievable. The purposes are as follows:

* the survival of the company as a going concern in whole or in part;
* the approval of a voluntary arrangement under Part 1 of the Act (see above);
* the sanctioning of a scheme of arrangement under s 425 of the Companies Act 1985 between the company and such persons as are mentioned in that section;
* a more advantageous realisation of the company's assets than would be effected on a winding up.

If an application for an administration order is made, none of the following may occur:

* no resolution may be passed or order made to wind the company up;
* no steps can be taken to enforce any security of the company's property or to repossess goods in the company's possession under any hire purchase agreement (this includes leasing agreements and retention of title agreements) except with the leave of the court and subject to such terms as it may impose;
* no other proceedings and no execution or other legal process may be commenced or continued and no distress levied against the company or its property except with the leave of the court and, once again, subject to such terms as it may impose.

If the court makes the order, then any petition for winding up the company shall be dismissed and any administrative receiver in place must vacate office. Whilst an administration order is in force, no resolution to wind the company up can be passed, no administrative receiver may be appointed and no steps may be taken to enforce any security of the company's property or to repossess goods in the company's possession under any hire purchase agreement except with the consent of the administrator or the leave of the court and subject to such terms as the court may impose.

The administrator should require a statement of affairs (p 119) to be made to him by those who have been running the company. He then drafts his own proposals for achieving the purpose or purposes set out in the order for the appointment of the administrator, laying a copy of the statement before a meeting of the company's creditors. He should also send a copy of the statement to all members of the company or publish it in the prescribed manner, setting out the address to which members should write for copies of the statement to be sent to them free of charge.

During the currency of an administration, s 27 of the Insolvency Act 1986 provides that a creditor or member may apply to the court for an order on the ground that the company's affairs, business or property are being or have been managed in a manner which is unfairly prejudicial to the interests of its creditors or members generally or some part of them or that any act or proposed act or omission of the administrator is or would be so prejudicial.

The provisions in the Insolvency Act 1986 relating to fair dealing (transactions at an undervalue) (s 238), preferences (s 239), extortionate credit transactions (s 244) and the invalidity of certain floating charges (s 245) apply to administration as they apply to liquidation.

Liquidation

There are essentially two types of winding up. There is compulsory winding up which is by court order and voluntary winding up which is initiated by the members of the company. Voluntary winding up may be further split into two types:

- a member's voluntary winding up, largely under the control of the members where the directors swear a statutory declaration of solvency; and
- creditors' voluntary winding up, largely under the control of the creditors where the directors have failed to swear a statutory declaration of solvency.

Compulsory liquidation

Section 122(1) of the Insolvency Act 1986 sets out the various grounds for compulsory winding up. They are as follows:

- the company has by special resolution resolved that the company be wound up by the court;
- the company is a public company which is registered as such on initial incorporation but has not been issued with a certificate to do business under s 117 of the Companies Act 1985 and more than a year has elapsed since it was so registered;
- the company is an old public company within the meaning of the Companies (Consequential Provisions) Act 1985;
- the company has not commenced business within a year of incorporation or suspends business for a year;
- the number of members is reduced to below two unless it is a private company to which the exemption relating to membership of one now applies;
- the company is unable to pay its debts;
- the court is of the opinion that it is just and equitable that the company should be wound up.

The last two grounds are the most important.

A company is unable to pay its debts if the conditions in s 123 of the Insolvency Act are satisfied. Inability to pay debts is demonstrated by one of the following:

- if a creditor is owed a debt exceeding £750 for three weeks after making a written request for payment of that debt;
- execution or process issued for payment on a judgment is returned unsatisfied in whole or in part (in practice the minimum sum owed must exceed £750);
- if it is proved to the satisfaction of the court that the company is unable to pay its debts as they fall due (in practice the same minimum sum applies);
- if the company's assets are worth less than the amount of its liabilities, taking account of contingent and prospective liability (in practice the same minimum sum applies);
- in Scotland a charge for payment on an extract decree or extract registered bond or extract registered process has expired without payment being made (in practice the same minimum sum applies).

The last ground set out in s 122 (just and equitable winding up) has been considered above.

In a compulsory winding up, if the case is made out, the petition may be granted. The commencement date of the liquidation is the date that the petition is presented, ie retrospectively the date of the commencement of liquidation is the date of the petition. This date is important for the calculation of time limits, eg for the fair dealing provisions of the Insolvency Act 1986.

Once a winding up petition has been presented, then any disposition of the company's property and any transfer of shares or alteration of its status is void unless the court orders otherwise.

Where a winding up order is granted, the court will appoint a provisional liquidator and that liquidator will be the official receiver (s 136(2) of the Insolvency Act 1986).

Separate meetings of creditors and contributories will be called for the purpose of choosing a permanent liquidator. The creditors and the contributories (the members) at their respective meetings may nominate a person to be liquidator and nominate representatives to a liquidation committee. The liquidator will generally be the person nominated by the creditors in the event of a conflict. The same meetings may nominate people to a liquidation committee. The purpose of the liquidation committee will be to liaise with the liquidator during the course of a winding up.

A statement of affairs is usually required by the official receiver.

Voluntary liquidation

Voluntary liquidation may commence in the following ways:

- if a fixed period has been settled for the duration of the company and the fixed period has now elapsed, then the company may be wound up by ordinary resolution;
- if the company resolves to be wound up voluntarily by a special resolution;
- if the company resolves by extraordinary resolution to be wound up on the basis that it cannot by reason of its liabilities continue its business (s 84 of the Insolvency Act 1986).

If the directors of the company or a majority of them swear to the effect that the company will be able to pay its debts in full together with interest within the next 12 months, then this represents a statutory declaration of solvency (s 89 of the Insolvency Act 1986). Where there is such a declaration, the liquidation will proceed as a members' voluntary winding up. The interests of the creditors are supposedly protected by the statutory declaration of solvency.

Where this is the case there will be a general meeting of members to pass a resolution to wind up and to appoint somebody as liquidator. In such a situation there is no liquidation committee.

If there is no statutory declaration of solvency, then the liquidation proceeds as a creditors' voluntary winding up. Here, general meetings of contributories and creditors will be convened. Each will nominate a liquidator but if there is a conflict, the creditors' choice will prevail. Once again, there will be a liquidation committee made up of equal numbers of representatives of the creditors and of the contributories.

A statement of affairs is made by the directors.

Progress of the liquidation

In every liquidation, the role of the liquidator is to get in the assets belonging to the company, to realise them and to pay off creditors in due order of priority. The priorities will be as follows:

- the fees and expenses of the liquidation, including the remuneration of the liquidator;
- the fixed charges will be paid off next;
- preferential creditors – preferential creditors are set out in Schedule 6 of the Insolvency Act 1986; they include any PAYE contributions that should have been deducted in the previous 12 months but have not been paid over, customs and excise dues for six months prior to liquidation and salary owing to employees for four months prior to liquidation up to a maximum of £800 per employee plus any accrued holiday pay;
- after preferential creditors are paid off, floating chargeholders will be paid off;
- ordinary trade creditors will be paid off next; also at this stage, any preferential creditors who are still owed money once the preference is exhausted, eg employees may be owed £1,000 back salary in which case £200 is non-preferential, will also be able to claim within this category;
- deferred debts are paid next; this is not an important category but within it are included dividends that are declared but not paid;

- if there are still assets available after all these creditors are paid off, capital is then returned to the members with regard to class rights. This may well occur since not all liquidations involve insolvency.

Priorities in a liquidation

Examination questions and generally problem questions arise frequently on priorities in a liquidation. In order to be able to tackle such questions, the examination candidate should be familiar with the provisions relating to registration of charges, provisions on reservation of title clauses, the law of liens, and the fair dealing provisions of the Insolvency Act 1986.

Most charges are registrable. They only enjoy priority as charges if properly registered. Failure to register does not, of course, affect the validity of the debt, merely the validity of the security. Section 396 of the Companies Act 1985 sets out the categories of charges that are registrable. The categories include all floating charges and most fixed charges. Charges are registrable within 21 days of their creation or acquisition. Failure to register a charge created by the company within the 21 day period may mean that the charge is void against an administrator or liquidator or any person acquiring an interest in or right over property subject to the charge. However, where a company acquires property already subject to a charge, failure to register will not affect the validity of such a charge, it will only render the company and any officer in default liable to a fine.

There is provision for late delivery of particulars under s 400 of the Companies Act 1985. Late registration is possible without application to the court (before the Companies Act 1989 amended the law, an application to the court was necessary). Section 401 permits delivery of further particulars to supplement or vary the registered particulars. To the extent that registered particulars do not contain relevant information and are incomplete, then the charge is void to that extent.

In answering a question, therefore, careful consideration needs to be given as to whether or not the charge is valid. There may also be consideration of supervening invalidity under the fair dealing provisions considered below.

As between different categories of charge, floating charges rank behind fixed charges, even subsequent fixed charges. The only exception to this principle is where there is a negative pledge clause in the floating charge providing that the company cannot create any subsequent charge, fixed or floating, with priority over a floating charge. If this negative pledge provision is actually known by the subsequent chargeholder, then the fixed charge will take behind the floating charge (see *Wilson v Kelland* (1910)).

The Secretary of State has power in s 415(2) to require that amongst the particulars requiring registration should be a negative pledge provision. Should the minister require registration of this, then there will be constructive notice of such a provision under s 416 of the Act. In this circumstance, the rule of actual notice in *Wilson v Kelland* will be supplanted by a rule of constructive notice.

As between fixed charges over the same property, the first in point of time takes priority. As regards floating charges, where there is more than one floating charge generally the first floating charge will take priority over the second. This is, however, subject to an exception where the first floating charge leaves open the possibility of a subsequent floating charge taking priority and the second floating charge is over a lesser category of property than the first (see *Re Automatic Bottlemakers* (1926)).

The liquidator will need to ensure in seeking to harness the property of the company and paying off creditors in due order of priority that all of the apparent property that the company holds actually belongs to the company. In commercial practice now, it is not infrequently the case that suppliers will seek to reserve title in goods until they have been fully paid for. Such reservation of title clauses take their name from the case *Aluminium Industrie Vaassen BV v Romalpa Aluminium Ltd* (1976) – thankfully *Romalpa* clauses! If a supplier reserves full title to property and creates a fiduciary relationship between the supplier and the supplied and there is no admixture of the property concerned, then title to the property will remain with the supplier until the goods have been fully paid for. This was what transpired in *Romalpa* itself. It is worth recalling, however, that *Romalpa* suffered from the reservation of title clause in the other party's terms of business!

In subsequent cases, the principle has been applied. In *Borden (UK) Ltd v Scottish Timber Products Ltd* (1979), there was a mixture of resin (in which title had been reserved) and chipboard. In such circumstances, there could be no effective reservation of title.

In *Re Bond Worth Ltd* (1979), we have an object lesson in how not to draft a reservation of title clause. The supplier sought only to reserve beneficial title to the goods. In such circumstances, the terms of business will necessarily imply that legal ownership has passed and, therefore, the supplier has merely created a charge which is registrable. The reservation of title clause was, therefore, held invalid in *Re Bond Worth Ltd*.

An interesting decision on reservation of title clauses is to be found in *Hendy Lennox (Industrial Engines) Ltd v Grahame Puttick Ltd* (1984). In this case, the supplier of diesel engines sought to reserve title to the engines. The engines were installed into generators. The court held that reservation was effective here since although the engines were installed into the generators they were not inextricably linked with them and the engines could be removed.

As well as knotty problems on reservation of title clauses, the examiner sometimes slips in a lien. A lien for these purposes exists where a person does work on property, eg repairing cars or machinery. The person performing the work has a lien over the property which he has worked upon until paid for his work. Where a company goes into liquidation and property is held by somebody in such a situation the liquidator cannot take the property until he has paid the fee (see *George Barker (Transport) Ltd v Eynon* (1974)).

Charges may be invalid under certain provisions in the Insolvency Act 1986, commonly known as the fair dealing provisions. Floating charges may, for example, be held invalid under s 245 of the Insolvency Act 1986. A floating charge created in favour of a connected person within a period of two years before the onset of insolvency is invalid except to the extent that it made for good consideration or within 12 months of the insolvency if it is made in favour of an unconnected person. If it is made in favour of an unconnected person, it also needs to be demonstrated that at the time the charge was created the company was unable to pay its debts. In *Re Shoelace* (1993), the Court of Appeal considered that a floating charge was within the scope of s 245 unless the consideration for which it was made is contemporaneous (*de minimis* excepted) (see Ferran (1994) CLJ 37).

Both fixed and floating charges may be caught by s 239 of the Insolvency Act 1986 if they constitute a preference. A charge will constitute a preference if it is unfairly preferring some creditors over others. The time periods here are two years where the person in whose favour it is created is a connected person and six months if the person is unconnected. The period concerned culminates with the onset of insolvency.

In addition to consideration of the provisions on registration of charges and possible invalidity of charges together with the reservation of title and lien considerations, a candidate should be familiar with the priority of payment.

First, the liquidator is able to claim for his remuneration and the expenses of the liquidation.

The next payment is to the beneficiaries of a fixed charge, or fixed charges if there is more than one fixed charge.

Preferential creditors are paid off next. Preferential creditors are identified in Schedule 6 of the Insolvency Act 1986. The categories rank equally and are as follows:

- PAYE contributions due in the 12 months before liquidation commences;
- VAT which is due for the six-month period before liquidation;
- car tax due in the 12-month period before liquidation;
- general betting duty, bingo duty and pool betting duty payable in the 12-month period before liquidation;
- NIC contributions which are due for the 12-month period before liquidation;
- any sums owing to occupational and state pension schemes;
- wages due to employees for the four-month period before liquidation up to £800 per employee;
- any accrued holiday pay owed to employees.

Note

Any sum advanced by a bank etc for paying salaries and accrued holiday pay which would otherwise have been preferential becomes preferential by subrogation.

After these preferential creditors have been paid off, the beneficiaries of floating charges are paid off next.

Ordinary unsecured trade creditors are paid off thereafter. Also within this category would be any person who has a preferential claim but whose preferential claim does not extend to all of the debt, eg an employee who is owed £1,000 back salary (£200 would be non-preferential).

After ordinary trade creditors are paid off, deferred creditors are paid off. The only important category of a deferred debt is a dividend which has been declared but not yet paid.

After this, if there still a surplus of assets (which may well be the case as many liquidations are solvent ones), then capital is returned to members in accordance with their class rights. Candidates are warned that often the examiner plays a mean trick and mixes questions on priority and liquidation with questions of class rights.

The provisions of the Companies Act 1989 on registration of charges, debentures etc have not yet been brought into force. The

Department of Trade and Industry has indicated that this part of the Act will be the subject of consultation in September 1994 as to possible future courses which will include bringing this part of the Act into force with amendments. The textbook is written on the basis that the provisions are in force.

Fair dealing provisions

In any liquidation and as has been seen in an administration, the fair dealing provisions of the Insolvency Act 1986 are of importance.

Section 238 of the Insolvency Act provides that an administrator or liquidator may apply to the court for an order of restitution where the company has entered into a transaction at an undervalue where the company makes a gift or receives significantly less consideration for a property than its true value. An order may be made if the transaction is in favour of a connected person within two years of the onset of insolvency, or if in favour of an unconnected person within six months of the onset of insolvency (this will be the date of the presentation of the petition if it is a compulsory winding up, or the date of the resolution if it is a voluntary winding up or the date of presentation of the petition to appoint an administrator in this case).

The same principle applies in relation to preferences. Preferring some creditors to others in the period before insolvency will constitute a preference. Thus, in *Re M Kushler Ltd* (1943), where a bank overdraft was paid off releasing a director's guarantee before liquidation, this was challenged under the old law where similar principles applied. This was successful.

Extortionate credit transactions, where creditors supply to the company on terms where the payments are grossly exorbitant or where the terms otherwise grossly contravene ordinary principles of fair dealing, are caught by s 244 of the Insolvency Act. Here the time limit is a three-year period terminating with the date of the administration order or the date when the liquidation commenced.

Section 245 of the Insolvency Act 1986 renders certain floating charges void. A floating charge created in favour of a connected person within the two years before the onset of insolvency is invalid except to the extent that it is made for good consideration or within 12 months of the onset of insolvency if it is made in favour of an unconnected person. If it is made in favour of an unconnected person, it also needs to be demonstrated that at the time the charge was created, the company was unable to pay its debts.

Malpractice

Another important area in relation to liquidation concerns penalisation of directors and officers for malpractice under s 212 of the Insolvency Act 1986. This covers the situation where the person who has been an officer, liquidator, administrator or administrative receiver or concerned in the promotion, formation or management of the company has misapplied or retained or become accountable for the company's money or property or has been guilty of any misfeasance or breach of any fiduciary or other duty in relation to the company.

Fraudulent trading

Section 213 of the Insolvency Act 1986 provides that the court may make an order for contribution to the company's assets where a person has traded fraudulently. Actual deceit must be proved but the section is not limited to officers of the company.

In the Insolvency Act 1985, now consolidated into s 214 of the Insolvency Act 1986, this was extended to wrongful trading where the director or shadow director ought to have known that the company could not pay its debts as they fell due. This welcome extension does not have a criminal counterpart (which the provision on fraudulent trading does have).

Wrongful trading

Section 214 of the Insolvency Act 1986 extends liability to directors or shadow directors who should know, or ought to have concluded, that there was no reasonable prospect that the company would avoid going into insolvent liquidation from the previous law which only penalised fraudulent trading where a person trading through the medium of the company actually knew that the company could not pay its debts. Section 214 therefore extends liability to the situation where a person ought to have realised that the company could not pay its debts. The section is, however, limited to directors and shadow directors. Furthermore, there is no criminal provision as there is for fraudulent trading (s 458 of the Companies Act 1985).

The provision on wrongful trading has 'altered the topography of company law' (Hicks, 14 *Company Lawyer* 16). As Prentice noted in

Creditors' Interests and Directors' Duties (1990) 'it is unquestionably one of the most important developments in company law this century'. The provision is important because it clearly strikes at the principle of limited liability established in *Salomon v A Salomon & Co Ltd* (1897). There are various reasons why claims for wrongful trading might be rare. First, it may not be easy to prove that a director ought to have known of the company's insolvency. Secondly, directors of companies may often themselves be in financial difficulty making it pointless for liquidators to pursue them. Furthermore, the uncertainty of a claim may be such that a liquidator is unwilling to risk creditors' funds in pursuing a wrongful trading claim (see Hicks above).

Significantly, wrongful trading is based upon an objective standard. Previously, directors' duties have tended to be a matter of subjective judgment (see *Re City Equitable Fire Insurance Co Ltd* (1925)).

The section was considered in *Re Produce Marketing Consortium Ltd (No 2)* (1989). In this case, the liquidator of the company sought an order under s 214 of the Insolvency Act 1986 against two directors. The auditors of the company which was in the business of importing fruit had warned the directors of the company's serious financial position. The judge found the directors liable to contribute £75,000. In determining how to decide whether the directors ought to have known of the company's position, Knox J had this to say:

The knowledge to be imputed in testing whether or not directors knew or ought to have concluded that there was no reasonable prospect of the company avoiding insolvent liquidation is not limited to the documentary material actually available at the given time. This appears from s 214(4) which includes a reference to facts which a director of a company not only should know but those which he ought to ascertain, a word which does not appear in s 214(2)(b). In my judgment this indicates that there is to be included by way of factual information not only what was actually there, but what, given reasonable diligence and an appropriate level of general knowledge, skill and experience, was ascertainable.

In *Re Purpoint Ltd* (1991), Vinelott J held a director of the company liable under the wrongful trading section where it should have been plain to him that the company could not avoid going into insolvent liquidation.

It has been suggested that banks which advance money to companies and then give directions to companies as to how to run their affairs where the companies are in financial difficulties may risk being held liable under the section. In *Re MC Bacon* (1990), a liquidator brought an action against a bank for wrongful trading as a shadow director. A shadow director is defined in s 741(2) of the Companies Act 1985 as:

... a person in accordance with whose directions or instructions the directors of the company are accustomed to act. However, a person is not deemed a shadow director by reason only that the directors act on advice given by him in a professional capacity.

On consideration of the matter as a preliminary issue Knox J refused to strike out a claim against the bank. He held that the claim could proceed. The matter did not proceed to trial but at the full trial Millett J considered the claim against the bank had been properly dropped. In *Re Hydrodan (Corby) Ltd* (1994), the question of wrongful trading once again appeared before Millett J. The company was a wholly owned subsidiary of Eagle Trust plc. The liquidator alleged that Eagle Trust, a subsidiary of Eagle Trust and the directors of Eagle Trust were liable for wrongful trading.

Millett J accepted that although the company had no active directors, although some directors were appointed, Eagle Trust could be a shadow director of the company. He held, however, that it did not follow that the directors of Eagle Trust were also shadow directors of the company. This would only be the case if the directors of Eagle Trust, who owed their duties to Eagle Trust, were in the practice of giving directions and instructions to the company which the company's directors acted upon.

Millett J held that the case had not been made out in the case before him.

The decision in *Re Hydrodan* is therefore illustrative of a restrictive approach to liability for wrongful trading and as noted by Bhattacharyya (15 *Company Lawyer* 151, 152), the decision is 'good news for banks'.

Developments in wrongful trading are clearly important, not just for questions on insolvency, but also in relation to questions of breaches of directors' duties. Section 214 has been used, for example, by Hoffmann J in *Norman v Theodore Goddard* (1991) in developing an objective standard of care and skill for directors. It was also employed by the same judge sitting as Hoffmann LJ in *Re D'Jan of London Ltd* (1993).

Take-overs, reconstructions and amalgamations

Take-overs

Sections 428–30F of the Companies Act 1985 provide for the compulsory acquisition of shares where the offeror acquires 90% of the shares of a target company. The acquisition of the minority holding will be ordered on the same terms as the majority was acquired. Not only does the majority have a right to acquire the minority, but the minority has a corresponding right to be acquired.

Schemes of arrangement

Sections 425–27A provide for schemes of arrangement. A scheme of arrangement would be made between the company and its creditors or members. The provisions are usually utilised where there is an internal reconstruction. The procedure involves application to the court with the proposed plan. If the proposed plan is legal, then the court will order meetings of the members and creditors as appropriate. If the meetings give the required consent by 75% in value of shares or debts, then this is reported back to the court which will then sanction the scheme if satisfied that the required consent is given. It may be seen that this procedure is relatively costly.

Amalgamation

A procedure for merger is offered by the Insolvency Act 1986 somewhat incongruously. If a company goes into voluntary liquidation, then the liquidator may accept shares from a transferee company in exchange for assets of the company. The shares of the transferee company are then distributed to the former members of the transferor company. A dissentient member of the transferor company can, however, insist on his interest being purchased for cash. This is one drawback with the procedure.

City Code on Take-overs and Mergers

Where a take-over involves a quoted company, the City Code on Take-overs and Mergers is the most crucial document. The code does not have the force of law but is policed by the City Panel on Take-overs and Mergers. The City Code is made up of general principles and detailed rules governing the conduct of the take-overs. It is updated from time to time.

There are also Stock Exchange rules governing the substantial acquisition of shares as well as provisions in the Companies Act designed to prevent a take-over by stealth (ss 198–219 of the Companies Act 1985).

Index